THE COURT-MARTIAL
OF CLAYTON LONETREE

The
COURT-MARTIAL
Of
CLAYTON
LONETREE

LAKE HEADLEY
with William Hoffman

A Donald Hutter Book

HENRY HOLT and COMPANY
New York

Published by Henry Holt and Company, Inc., 115 West 18th Street, New York,
New York 10011.
Published in Canada by Fitzhenry & Whiteside Limited, 195 Allstate Parkway,
Markham, Ontario L3R 4T8.

Library of Congress Cataloging-in-Publication Data
Headley, Lake.
The court-martial of Clayton Lonetree / Lake Headley with William
Hoffman. — 1st ed.
    p.   cm.
"A Donald Hutter book."
ISBN 0-8050-0893-4
1. Lonetree, Clayton, 1961– —Trials, litigation, etc. 2. Trials (Espionage)—
Virginia—Quantico. 3. Courts-martial and courts of inquiry—United States. I.
Hoffman, William, 1937– . II. Title.
KF7642.L66H43   1989
343.73′0143—dc19
[347.303143]   89-1776
                                                                                                CIP

Henry Holt books are available at special discounts for bulk purchases for sales
promotions, premiums, fund-raising, or educational use. Special editions or book
excerpts can also be created to specification.

For details contact:

Special Sales Director
Henry Holt and Company, Inc.
115 West 18th Street
New York, New York 10011

First Edition

Designed by A. Christopher Simon
Printed in the United States of America

10   9   8   7   6   5   4   3   2   1

To my sons and best friends,
Anthony and Rod Headley,
and especially Lake III, who has lived this
and many other cases,
always solidly there at my side
through some very trying times.

Thanks are due Judy Hoffman, continuing to work when everyone else tired; our editor, Don Hutter, who worked long and brilliantly bringing the book to fruition; Marjorie, Kathleen, and Michael Stirling; Dr. Nicholas G. and Becky Behnen; Mark and Jeanene Behnen; William, Joe, Terri, and John Hoffman; Terry Lee Headley; Bill Helmer; Tammy Headley; Donald and Patty Freed; Dominic P. Gentile; John and Anita Reeves; Bill Gibbs; Ola Graney; Mike and Roxanne Wysocki; Jon and Glynna Robinson; Charles Ced; Rudy Ced; Betty Duke; George and Nancy Vlassis; Carter Camp; Lea, Ethan, and Micah Lewis; Carol and Dewey Belvin; Jeff German; Jerry Shields; Jerry Kelly; Phil Hershkop; Billy Dean Smith; Jim Stanley; Mike and Paul Stuhff and family; Ken Franks; and Oliver.

CONTENTS

Part Three: Court-Martial

INTRODUCTION

By William M. Kunstler[1]

Reading Lake Headley's *The Court-Martial of Clayton Lonetree*
revived for me scores of poignant memories of our mutual participation in this most tragic of cases. The long months we spent
together at Quantico, Virginia, as part of the defense team for
this beleaguered Marine sergeant not only made us both think
back to our days as members of the Wounded Knee Legal De-
fense/Offense Committee (WKLDOC) in South Dakota fifteen
years earlier, but starkly reminded us that injustice toward Native
Americans is hardly limited to any particular time or place. Sergeant Lonetree was every bit as brutally victimized as were the
residents of the Pine Ridge Indian Reservation who, in early 1973,
aided by the American Indian Movement, seized and held the
symbolic hamlet of Wounded Knee in order to dramatize their
wholly justified grievances.

When Sergeant Lonetree came forward around Christmastime
of 1986 to reveal to the authorities in Vienna, Austria, where he
was then stationed, that his brief love affair with a Soviet national,

[1]Vice-President and Volunteer Staff Attorney, Center for Constitutional Rights,
New York, NY.

who had worked as a receptionist in the American Embassy in Moscow, his last post, had thrown him into contact with KGB operatives, he furnished what a high-ranking CIA official later characterized as extremely valuable information as to the identities of several key Russian agents. Instead of being appropriately appreciative, the Naval Investigative Service (NIS) conspired with the CIA and the State Department in a massive effort to execute him in order to insulate the Reagan Administration against wholly legitimate charges of longstanding and abominably lax security measures at the Moscow Embassy. When indecent efforts to implicate him in an alleged scheme with another minority member of the Marine Security Guard to permit Soviet agents to enter and roam freely about the building failed, thus eliminating the possibility of imposing the death penalty, the government sought, and eventually obtained, a savage thirty-year sentence. The vile tactics employed to reach this plateau are dramatically and eloquently revealed in Lake's gripping book.

In his punishment-stage summation to the all-officer jury, the prosecutor kept hammering on the theme that Lonetree was the only Marine in the Corps' more-than-200-year history ever to be charged with espionage. In actuality, this was not so. Between 1982 and 1986, at least four other Marines had been accused of a number of espionage-related crimes of far more serious implication than the Lonetree charges, both in the United States and overseas, and in unpublicized prosecutions (as opposed to the Lonetree court-martial) were ultimately given sentences of two years or less.

Although these other cases are not, quite properly, included in Lake's book, the fact does go to prove his principal thesis, namely that Lonetree was singled out for special and draconian treatment, possibly because he was an American Indian who had supposedly stained the escutcheon of an historically white military organization, but certainly to place on his shoulders the collective guilt of others, many in the highest of places.

Clayton Lonetree, stripped of his hard-won sergeant's stripes, sits today in the Leavenworth, Kansas, service prison, enduring his awful sentence, understandably bitter and confused over the way the white man's government has treated him. I can only hope that Lake's book will be of some small comfort to him and that the crawling appellate process will, some day, undo, as much as it realistically can, the enormous injustices visited upon him. *Semper Fidelis* may be the motto of the Marine Corps, but it hardly applied to the inhumane and vindictive vendetta against one of its own, one who was perhaps, in the last analysis, more faithful to its traditions than were those who prosecuted and judged him.

THE COURT-MARTIAL
OF CLAYTON LONETREE

PROLOGUE

The name of the key prosecution witness in the court-martial of Sgt. Clayton John Lonetree—a twenty-six-year-old Native American and the first U.S. Marine to be publicly tried for espionage—remains unknown to those of us who composed his defense team. In fact there is hardly anything we do know about the man. We were not permitted, either in pretrial deposition or during his two-hour appearance on the stand, to question him on his professional background or in any way to test his credibility as a witness.

As William Kunstler, Lonetree's civilian co-defense counsel, incredulously pointed out, this was the first time in the history of U.S. criminal law that a witness testified in a major court case without giving his name and without the accused being given the right, granted by the Sixth Amendment to the U.S. Constitution, "to be confronted with the witnesses against him." It was a right which thousands of courts before this one had interpreted as allowing the accused to establish the identity and credentials of his accusers, and to cross-examine them as to the veracity of their testimony.

There was no way for us to show whether this court-declared

"John Doe," the U.S. Navy's only alleged witness to have identified Lonetree's supposed KGB contact, was lying or was simply an out-and-out fraud.

Sitting in that makeshift courtroom at Quantico, Virginia, on the twenty-eighth day of Clayton's court-martial—August 27, 1987—I felt violently ill, sick to my stomach with frustration at this latest violation of his constitutional rights. I had a special reason for my anger. More than anyone else in that crowded, hot room—actually a basement office on the Quantico Marine base hastily converted for what had become one of the most publicized trials in U.S. military jurisprudence—I *knew* that John Doe was a liar. A professional CIA liar.

Just the day before, as chief investigator for the defense, I had conducted a pretrial interview of John Doe. In his late fifties, six feet tall, heavy-set with a puffy face, small hands, and gray hair not quite long enough to give him a hippyish look, he had sat across from me in a Quantico office flanked by CIA and State Department lawyers.

I asked him: "Are you told during your training that at certain times you must lie?"

"Yes."

"Under oath?"

"Sometimes."

"How do we know you'll tell the truth during this court-martial?"

"Well, I will."

"But you've been told there are times for you to lie under oath?"

"Yes."

"But you'll tell the truth at the court-martial?"

"Yes."

"How can I be sure?"

"Because I'm telling you."

"But you could have been told to lie to *me*?"

"Yes."

"How am I supposed to know when you tell the truth?"

"Because I'm telling you."

"But you might lie about that?"

"Yes."

Doe was admitting he *might* lie while saying that he *would* tell the truth. Which itself might be a lie. Alice in Wonderland, yet another charade in a trial that had long since become a travesty of justice.

I stared at Doe before turning to something more substantial. On December 26, 1986, Doe had supposedly made an appearance at a site in Vienna for a meeting that Clayton, then under arrest, *but not realizing he was under arrest,* had reported scheduling with a KGB officer, a man named Yuriy Lysov but known to Clayton only by his code name of "George." The defense knew Doe would testify that indeed George showed up for the appointment. Transcripts of tape recorded statements Lonetree had unwittingly made to agents of the Naval Investigative Service (NIS) filled more than 250 almost marginless, closely spaced pages, yet Doe was the prosecution's only corroboration.

Doe described George to me as a man in his late fifties, five feet eleven inches, approximately 165 pounds—"hard to tell because he wore a hat and coat"—with gray hair.

"What kind of hair?" I asked.

"Like mine. A full head of white hair."

"How do you know George had a full head of hair if he wore a hat? And how do you know it was white?"

Many men with white sideburns have dark hair, a fact that Doe shrugged off when I pointed it out to him.

As we went on, I got the distinct feeling that Doe was getting uncomfortable about his "observance" of George. Not that he had anything to worry about, knowing as he did that there would be no way the defense could dispute him.

He told me he had observed George—identified from a twenty-year-old photograph—pacing in front of St. Wenceslaus Church, at night, during a blowing snowstorm, for one and a half seconds. Doe said he got another two and a half seconds of viewing time after hailing a cab and driving back past the subject.

I'd had an artist use that same photo of George to sketch how he might look twenty years later. Four different faces emerged.

Anticipating that any background on Doe relative to the case would be quashed in court "for national security purposes," I tried to learn what I could about this anonymous star witness. A U.S.

citizen, he'd been a "soldier in the U.S. Army" and had taught in high school before his twenty-five-year service in the CIA, twenty of those years spent working undercover in Europe. He claimed to make over fifty I.D.'s a year, "perhaps thirty from photos," and said the government sent him to Vienna specifically for the purpose of eyeballing George.

"Were any photographs taken of George in front of St. Wenceslaus Church?" I asked him, knowing that this was standard operating procedure for the CIA when gathering evidence for government cases.

"No," Doe answered.

"Why not?"

"Too obvious. Too risky."

I didn't believe him. Too obvious with all the opportunities of concealed vantage around St. Wenceslaus Church? Too risky given CIA methods and technology for surreptitious photography? No, I figured, they had taken a photograph, all right, but they couldn't be sure whether it actually showed Yuriy Lysov alias George. And if it didn't, if it could be shown in court that the subject might be someone else, any such admission would force an immediate dismissal of all charges against Lonetree.

"Were any other agents present when you observed George in front of St. Wenceslaus?"

"No."

Again, as with the question of the photograph of George, was this an instance of Doe having been told to lie? Through the discovery process I had obtained pictures of the intersection where George had allegedly stood. The pictures were marked with three X's and had captions indicating that the X's represented positioned agents, one of them a woman. The CIA had given me the wrong set of photographs! When they realized their mistake they demanded them back (promising to give me instead a set of unmarked, uncaptioned photographs which, they made clear, were the ones they had originally intended to give me and the only ones that would be introduced in evidence). I complied, but not before making copies of the first set. With those copies in hand, the defense then applied to the court to call the other two agents— James Doe and Jane Doe?—to testify. Military Judge Capt. Philip

Roberts, the officer presiding over the Lonetree court-martial, had ruled that only *John* Doe would be heard.

I asked Doe, "And you saw George just this once, for about four seconds total?"

"Oh, no, there was a second time, a few days later, in a park."

Perhaps the whole incredible case—filled with declared agents, concealed agents, and alias-using agents, while everyone else from minor officials in the Moscow and Vienna embassies to the Secretary of Defense was playing that favorite bureaucratic game known as Cover Your Ass—had made me cynical, but I didn't buy John Doe's second observance. Just as I hadn't bought the first.

"Tell me about this second time."

"Like I said, it was at a park."

"What did George wear?"

"A heavy coat. And a cap like British race-car drivers wear."

I suspected Doe was sensing trouble with his full-head-of-white-hair description. Back then the freezing cold temperatures would have chilled Vienna, so Doe couldn't very well describe George as bareheaded; a cap was a nice compromise between cover-up and visibility.

"How did you know George was going to be in the park?"

"For reasons of national security I can't tell you that."

"What can't you tell me?"

"I tried to appear as inconspicuous as possible. I feared being recognized. I had a dog with me, so I looked like I was just taking a walk."

"Was it your dog?"

"No. The animal belongs to someone else."

"A CIA dog?"

"No. I borrowed him from a friend."

"Was the dog briefed on the mission?"

"Huh?"

"Did the dog have a top-secret clearance?"

I was baiting Doe, trying to get him angry enough to blurt out something valuable, anything to shake his recorded deposition testimony. ("I'm sick of you, wiseguy. There was no goddamn dog, and we both know it.") Doe's face did get red and he glared at me evilly, but with effort he reined himself in. One of the government lawyers suggested I get more serious. I'd never been more serious in my life.

Later, one of those two lawyers who had accompanied Doe through the interview paid me the compliment of telling chief defense counsel Michael Stuhff that he should count himself fortunate to have me as an investigator. "Best piece of questioning I've ever heard," he said.

The compliment was small comfort for what happened the next day when Doe testified at the court-martial, when he stunned the other members of the defense into their own disbelief by suddenly remembering a *third* observance of George. This time Doe had sat "five feet away" from the subject, indoors . . . and therefore could tell that George indeed had white hair.

"Why a third observation?" Stuhff asked in the courtroom.

"It was on another matter."

"What other matter?"

"I respectfully refuse to answer on the grounds of national security."

The rest of the questioning that day, aside from the predictable exchanges over Doe's observances of George, went like this:

STUHFF: Where were you born, Mr. Doe?

DOE: I respectfully refuse to answer on the grounds of national security.

STUHFF: For whom do you work, Mr. Doe?

DOE: I respectfully refuse to answer on the grounds of national security.

And so on.

Anyone obtaining a copy of Clayton Lonetree's court-martial transcript can learn nothing from reading John Doe's testimony. Almost everything is whited out. For example, the following is all that remains on four of the forty-nine pages (fifty-one lines each) devoted to questions directed to and answers by John Doe:

Swarms of reporters attending from all over the globe never caught a glimpse of John Doe. The media were outside the courtroom. Forced to cover the trial via closed-circuit television from a house atop a hill some two hundred yards removed from the actual proceedings, they faced an impossible task as TV monitors faded to black during critical testimony. They never even heard the "Uhs" and "Uh-huhs." And as soon as Doe's testimony was finished he was hustled out of the courtroom the same way he had been hustled in: Joseph Valachi-style through a side entrance.

By now burning with frustration and anger, I left the courtroom right after Doe, knowing that he had handed the desperate prosecution just the corroboration needed to secure a conviction. Mike Stuhff joined me and noticed my glum expression. "There's one positive, Lake," he said.

"What's that?"

"If Doe's testimony and what they wouldn't let us do with him in there don't count as grounds for a mistrial, then nothing ever will."

Perhaps. But then there was Clayton, a young man I'd come to know very well, and to like, for all the delusions that still gripped his susceptible mind. How long would he be forced to languish in a Marine brig, as he had now for eight months, before any such appeal might set him free?

And what till then? I wondered. What chance might he still have with this court? Clayton had spent his entire life waiting for something good to happen.

PART ONE

Clayton and His Crimes

1

THE MAKING OF A SCAPEGOAT

My familiarity with Clayton Lonetree's childhood and his years in the Marines comes from many sources and conversations over the course of my extensive background checks as investigator for his defense, not only with Clayton—who gave me as well his own full account of his actions in Moscow and Vienna—but also with close relatives and others able to recall the shy, quiet, and unassuming Native American before his notoriety as an alleged traitor to his country.

The tracks of that woefully unsettled childhood—shuttling between parents and among family friends, back and forth over a wide swath of the American heartland—were sometimes faint and difficult to follow, but the omens they offered of an inevitably scarred and troubled young man ran deep and unmistakable.

His life began in Chicago, where he was born on November 6, 1961, to unmarried parents—to Spencer Lonetree, twenty-one, a Winnebago, and Sally Tsosie, sixteen, a Navajo.

Sally had ventured to Chicago from the Intermountain School in Brigham, Utah, looking for work. She met Spencer, a musician playing in local bands, dated him, and in time moved with him to Lake Dalton, Wisconsin, where she became pregnant. The couple quarreled often. Lack of money was a constant problem, but for Sally the main issue was Spencer's continual criticism of her lack of education, which she maintained he held up as the reason he would never marry her. The couple separated, Spencer moving to the nearby town of Wisconsin Dells and Sally returning to Chicago, where she moved in with a friend and found work as a film librarian to support herself until she came to term. Spencer learned of Clayton's birth a few days after the fact and hurried the 220 miles to Chicago to see his son. The new parents agreed to give the relationship another chance. They moved into a small apartment on Chicago's north side, an area to which Native Americans regularly migrate in hope of finding jobs.

Sally still had her job as film librarian, and she was back to it within a week of delivering Clayton. So the task of taking care of her son fell largely to Spencer. It was a reversal of roles unusual for Native Americans, and by the time Sally gave birth to a second son, Craig, on August 8, 1963, her relations with Spencer had deteriorated hopelessly. She resented his drinking and what she considered his unwarranted jealousy and verbal abuse. She particularly remembers Spencer blaming her for Craig's cleft palate.

Spencer decided the time had come to "put some distance" between himself and Sally, and left his family. At first Sally, almost equally eager to put more distance between herself and Spencer, took the boys to her ancestral Navajo reservation at Big Mountain, Arizona. But then, in 1965, desperate to obtain surgery for Craig's cleft palate, she returned to Chicago. That December the operation was indeed performed, and Clayton also underwent surgery to correct protruding ears. Sally paid for both operations with meager savings and help from concerned friends.

By then Spencer was making occasional brief reappearances, sometimes taking Clayton with him when he left. (Sally gave birth in 1966 to a daughter, Valerie, but Spencer denies being the father.) In the summer of 1966, Clayton, age five, was living with his father in Wisconsin Dells and performing the hoop dance for tourists at the Stand Rock Indian ceremonial. As a singer and featured hoop dancer, Spencer impressed the audience using five rings while little Clayton performed with three.

The situation grew worse the end of that summer when Spencer married Virginia Rollinger from North St. Paul, Minnesota, and the couple, with Clayton in tow, moved to Chicago where Spencer found work. Sally, who had welcomed Spencer's latest attempt to "put distance" between them, now found herself living in the same city, Spencer with another woman as well as her own oldest son.

Lack of money continued to be a problem for both parents, and finally in late 1966, Sally initiated proceedings for custody of Clayton and child support. Spencer was arrested, taken to jail, and the next day a judge ruled in favor of Sally's custody suit and ordered Spencer to pay seventy-five dollars a month for each son.

This hardly settled the matter. In June, 1967, Spencer came by and whisked both his sons out of Chicago, leaving them with a sister in Kenosha while he and Virginia completed arrangements for a move into a mobile home in Wisconsin Dells.

That summer Clayton again performed the hoop dance at the Stand Rock Indian Ceremonial, and Virginia gave birth to Spencer's daughter, whom they named Lisa.

Convinced that Spencer represented a disaster as a father, Sally plotted to get her sons back. But she needed time, a plan, and money.

In the summer of 1968 Virginia took Craig, then almost five, and Lisa to St. Paul to search for a permanent home. Clayton and his father remained in Wisconsin Dells through the summer. During the day the youngster was cared for by neighbors while his father worked, and at night he performed the hoop dance for tourists.

The family needed the money the six-year-old earned, but otherwise he was hardly taken into account. Lonely and confused, gawked at by strangers, Clayton had no close friends with whom to play. In fact throughout his childhood he never did make a close friend. Perhaps in Wisconsin Dells he had begun already to retreat into that dream world which in such large measure led to his eventual tragedy.

That fall Spencer enrolled the boys at the Longfellow Elementary School in St. Paul, Clayton in the first grade and Craig in kindergarten. The following January Virginia gave Spencer another son, Scott. Meanwhile, Spencer started going to school himself, and working nights.

In Chicago, Sally was making her plans. Through friends she arranged for a job on the Navajo reservation in New Mexico, then waited in Chicago for her opportunity.

In June, 1969, with his family again in dire need of money, Spencer took seven-year-old Clayton back to Wisconsin Dells to stay with a friend and two uncles, again to work as a hoop dancer.

As soon as she learned of this, Sally drove the four hundred miles to St. Paul and told Virginia that she wanted to take Craig on a vacation to Canada. At first Virginia objected, but unable to reach Spencer she reluctantly gave in. Having regained custody of her youngest boy, Sally made a beeline for Wisconsin Dells where Spencer had just deposited Clayton, grabbed her oldest son, and headed for New Mexico.

It was seven months before Spencer learned of his children's whereabouts. Immediately he went to New Mexico and confronted Sally, but when the boys convinced him they were content living with their mother, Spencer returned to St. Paul.

Early in 1970, Sally lost her job. Unable to support Clayton and Craig, and regarding it as unthinkable to return them to their father, Sally placed them in the Navajo Gospel Mission, a Baptist orphanage and school in Farmington, New Mexico. The Mission operated in the centuries-old tradition of Christianizing Native Americans—so often at the cost of their native culture and values.

Clayton learned discipline and fear of the Lord at the Navajo Gospel Mission. He also learned to obey orders and respect authority. All moral issues were black and white in the strict, no-nonsense world of the Mission. (It must have surprised the Mission's director, Reverend Jack Drake, when years later President Ronald Reagan cited Clayton's behavior at the U.S. Embassy in Moscow as representing "the fruit" of an American educational system which "shies away" from teaching "principles of what is right or what is wrong.")

Students at the Farmington school had surrogate mothers and fathers assigned to them, but the turnover of such "parents" was so rapid, Clayton never really got close to any adult. He continued to retreat inside himself, a loner without friends or mentors, conjuring elaborate fantasies increasingly divorced from the real world. But he was good at taking orders, like any good soldier. Presenting no disciplinary problems for his elders, Clayton soaked up the fundamental Baptists' bleak view of the world and came to consider himself a devout and principled Christian.

After leaving Craig and Clayton at the Mission school, Sally returned to Chicago, where she found work and, finally, a husband, Richard. That same year, 1970, Spencer and Virginia were divorced.

Sally had left the boys at the Mission with firm orders that they were not to be released to Spencer. In fact, Spencer remained unaware of their whereabouts until Christmas, 1971. Immediately he initiated custody proceedings on the grounds that their enrollment at the Gospel Mission had been without his approval and was harmful to their upbringing.

When Sally learned of Spencer's action early in 1972, she moved with Richard and their new daughter to Farmington and took Craig and Clayton out of the Navajo Gospel Mission. The family rented a house, Richard finding temporary work with an oil company and then what looked like a permanent job, with the City of Gallup, New Mexico, in construction. But within another six months he had lost the job, and the two boys were back in the Baptist school.

Spencer married again in 1973, and grew increasingly impatient with the slow pace of the custody proceedings. He fired his New Mexico lawyer, hired a Minnesota attorney, and when that failed to produce results, he decided simply to take the children, reasoning that, in line with his understanding of property cases, possession represented nine-tenths of the law.

A complicated plan involving a rental car and requiring coordination with Clayton and Craig leaked to school authorities, who prevented the "kidnapping."

A more straightforward approach, on Christmas Eve, 1974, brought success. Sally and Richard had by then moved to her ancestral home at Big Mountain, Arizona. When Spencer asked that his boys be allowed to spend the holiday with him and his new wife in St. Paul, and Craig seemed eager at the prospect (Clayton seldom expressed any preference), Sally agreed. Spencer simply never sent them back.

Shortly after the youngsters arrived, Spencer and his new wife, JoAnne, separated.

In the course of his four years at the Navajo Gospel Mission— living as one of ten children in a single cottage, often crying himself to sleep—Clayton had become convinced that his mother had abandoned him. Spencer did nothing to change that impression, though in time Clayton would look back on his years at the Mission as the *good part* of growing up.

With the boys, now ages thirteen and eleven, permanently in his keep, Spencer assumed the role of disciplinarian under a rekindled sense of parental responsibility, pushing them hard to strive for excellence. He supervised housecleaning and homework with an iron hand, and every morning before dawn he had the boys out jogging, even in the bitter Minnesota winter. Like a military drill sergeant, he called them "girls"—as in "Let's go, girls, shape up!"

"I wanted my sons to make it in the white world," Spencer says. "I wanted them to achieve and make something of their lives. I drove them hard. I told Clayton to shoot for becoming a U.S. Senator. I didn't want them using the fact they were Indians as a crutch."

Spencer's aim may have been to instill in his sons a sense of pride, of self-worth, but the effect on Clayton was a confusion of identity. As he would one day admit to me, Clayton thought of himself as an "apple," a deprecating Native American term similar to the Black word "oreo." An apple is red on the outside and white on the inside, where it counts.

Spencer's numerous pep talks might have inspired the youngsters more had they been delivered by a sober father, but Clayton's chief memory of those Minnesota years has Spencer drunk much of the time, boasting garrulously about his toughness—like the frequent story of how he earned the nickname "Charlie Potatoes" in barroom fights through Illinois, Wisconsin, New Mexico, and Minnesota.

Attending Johnson High School in St. Paul, Clayton stayed to himself and made no close friends, all the time striving mightily to impress Spencer. "He was backup quarterback," recalls Fred Brett, an assistant principal, "and that would characterize his life. He showed up and did well enough to make the team."

Clayton showed up because he was supposed to show up. Clayton always obeyed orders. He didn't miss a single day of school his first two years, pedaling his bicycle the ten-mile round trip through all kinds of weather. His perfect attendance record ended in his junior year, on his sixteenth birthday, when his father insisted that he and Craig participate in a fundraising marathon. Clayton might not have the speed to excel in sports, but he could run all day; his endurance was phenomenal, and he loved going off by himself on long jaunts. Thus he is remembered all the more as a "loner" by his fellow students and teachers, thinking of the shy Native American youngster today probably more than when he was among them.

Hardworking and persistent, Clayton continued trying to win his father's approval and to fulfill his father's ambition that he become "somebody." He took a part-time job at the Radisson Hotel in St. Paul during his junior year of high school, putting in more and more time until, between work and school, he was down to five hours sleep a night. Often, trying to catch up on his studies early in the morning, he'd fall asleep hunched over the kitchen table.

The management at the Radisson remembers Clayton as the ideal employee. He was neat, thorough, polite . . . and always did as he was told.

Clayton worked long, hard hours to impress his father, but he also wanted to be away from his drinking. Spencer wanted his son to go to college, but by the end of his junior year Clayton had decided to join the Marine Corps for a better chance to get away from home.

Clayton's family had a long tradition of military service. Relatives had fought valiantly in virtually every conflict, from the Civil War to Vietnam, and one of them, a great-uncle named Mitchell Red Cloud, was one of America's great war heroes, winner of the Congressional Medal of Honor.

Clayton had heard the Mitchell Red Cloud story countless times, but his admiration of the legend only grew. In August 1941, Red Cloud received permission from his father to leave school and enlist in the Marine Corps. Assigned to the First Marine Division in the Pacific theater, he served with the renowned Carlson's Raiders until, during combat on Guadalcanal, he contracted malaria, losing eighty-five of his two hundred pounds, and was evacuated to the United States. Once recovered, Mitchell Red Cloud refused an honorable discharge, returned to the Pacific, and engaged in fierce action on Okinawa and the Ryukyu Islands.

The war ended and this time Red Cloud accepted an honorable discharge. But then, with the outbreak of the Korean War, he reenlisted and was soon back in combat.

Corporal Red Cloud's Medal of Honor citation, signed by President Harry Truman, describes the gallantry with which his life ended. He was serving in Company E of the 19th Infantry Regiment, guarding Hill 123 near Chonhyon. The citation reads, in part:

> From his position on the point of a ridge immediately in front of the company command post, he was the first to detect the approach of the Chinese Communist forces and give the alarm as the enemy charged from a brush covered area less than 100 feet from him.
>
> Springing up he delivered devastating point-blank automatic rifle fire into the advancing enemy. His accurate and intense fire checked the assault and gained time for the company to consolidate its defense.
>
> With utter fearlessness, he maintained his firing position until severely wounded by enemy fire. Refusing assistance, he pulled himself to his feet, and wrapping his arm around a tree, continued his deadly fire until he was again, and fatally, wounded.
>
> His heroic act stopped the enemy from overrunning his company's position and gained time for reorganization and evacuation of the wounded. Cpl. Red Cloud's dauntless courage and gallant self-sacrifice reflects the highest credit upon himself and upholds the esteemed traditions of the Army of the United States.

Clayton spent his senior year, 1979–80, working at the Radisson Hotel, reading extensively (history and current affairs absorbed him particularly), taking a course in German (indulging a fascination for languages that has never left him), and looking forward to getting away from St. Paul. He enlisted in the Marines just before graduation but was not scheduled to begin active duty until July 29. So upon graduation from Johnson High School, having saved several thousands of dollars from his years at the Radisson, he purchased a large backpack and hitchhiked to New Mexico to visit the Navajo Gospel Mission, by now fondly recalled, and to Arizona to see his mother.

During his two months in Farmington, Clayton fell in love for the first time. Her name was Nancy Snyder, she came from West Palm Beach, Florida, and she was visiting a sister who worked at the Mission school as a surrogate parent. Nancy and the would-be Marine hit it off from the start.

As she recalls, "We went for long walks, and we talked about how we were both bummed out on our parents. You know how you are as teenagers."

Nancy was especially impressed by Clayton's rapport with the children at the Mission. "He used to let them sit on his lap," she remembers, "and he'd push them in the swings. They all thought he walked on water." He could position himself right at their level, talk to them not as an older authority figure but as a concerned wiser friend. He tried to become for them what he felt his parents had never been for him.

Nancy Snyder provided other insights after the Lonetree case became a cause célèbre: "Clayton told me that he wished he were white. He said to me, 'I was raised white, but I'm not.' He was really not proud of being an Indian, and I told him he should be proud of his heritage. Clayton had a way of faking a sense of pride, but deep down he was insecure. I don't think I've ever met anyone so lonely."

Lonely *and* alone. Extremely shy, regarding himself as an unwanted child, he never opened up to other males his age. Yet always growing in his mind was the obsession of "being somebody."

Clayton and Nancy agreed to marry when she finished high school in Florida, and each promised not to date anyone else. She returned to her parents in West Palm Beach, made jewelry for Clayton in art class, wrote long letters. He telephoned her every Friday night, sounding extremely irritated whenever she wasn't home to answer. And there were other signs of a growing possessive jealousy.

The jealousy preyed on Nancy; she'd missed her senior prom because of him. When he came to Florida to visit, they walked on the beach and she told Clayton point-blank how she felt.

Tears came to Clayton's eyes. "I don't want you to ever leave me like my mother did," he said. "I'd kill myself."

Nancy Snyder joined the Marines upon graduation, hoping to serve at a base with Clayton. But soon after their engagement became official, the relationship chilled. Deeply insecure and inexperienced in intimate dealings with others, Clayton couldn't curb his possessive jealousy of Nancy. It lost him not only his fiancée but the one person in whom he could confide.

Clayton completed boot training in San Diego. The exhausting regimen proved less taxing on him than on most of the other recruits. His physical endurance was strong, and following orders without question or complaint came naturally. Spencer Lonetree's son had learned to face authority with a willing, almost docile, compliance. From my own military experience—serving with the 39th Infantry Regiment, 9th Infantry Division in the Army of Occupation at Nuremberg—I could picture Clayton impressing his Marine officers as an ideal soldier.

Clayton completed Infantry Training School at Camp Pendleton and served a one-year tour of duty at the Marine Barracks, Guantanamo Bay, Cuba. Mainly he kept his mouth shut, made no trouble, kept to himself, and pursued his interest in history and current affairs through extensive reading. Fellow Marines considered him "a good guy." Superiors thought him "a good Marine."

It was the start of an unblemished record as a Marine. Clayton was promoted to Private First Class on January 1, 1981; to Lance Corporal on September 1, 1981; Corporal on May 1, 1983; and Sergeant on February 1, 1985—four promotions in four years. His Military Occupational Speciality (MOS) was rifleman. Twice he earned the Good Conduct Medal, and once the Sea Service Deployment Ribbon.

A good soldier he might have been, and even an adequate sergeant, but he didn't possess the stuff of leadership. When he briefly commanded a squad of Marines, superiors found him too "easy," too "soft" on his men, and quickly replaced him. Clayton was very helpful to those under him, very patient with them, but more in the manner of a concerned older brother than as a leader of men.

Clayton was reassigned from Guantanamo Bay back to Camp Pendleton, and after a year he applied for duty with the elite Marine Security Guard Battalion. He had decided by now that his future was to be not with the Marines but with the State Department—that would be something, he thought, to become a Native American diplomat—and assignment to the MSG Battalion could help pave the way.

Sen. Rudy Boschwitz (D-Minn.) sponsored and endorsed his application, but Clayton failed the entrance tests. His grades in school had never been better than mediocre, and since graduation, despite all his reading, he hadn't acquired the broad-based knowledge needed to score well on intelligence examinations. He knew a lot about a few things—most of it raw historical information he could interpret only for himself, without benefit of such wider context or deeper understanding as a good teacher might have provided—and virtually nothing about others.

But Senator Boschwitz, impressed by the Native American's ambition, stuck by him, and on his second try Clayton passed the MSG exam. His Marine Corps superiors seemed delighted, and gave reason to believe that he would get one of the duty stations he had listed among his preferences. And he did: Moscow.

No more visible U.S. presence exists in foreign countries than the Marine Guards—138 U.S. embassies and consulates around the world are guarded by Marines—and this holds true especially in the capital of the Soviet Union. As much as the U.S. hammers away at Russia for human rights abuses, the USSR pounds back about mistreatment of Native Americans in this country. Native people like Leonard Peltier and Russell Means are heroes to the Soviet population, just as dissident Andrei Sakharov is to ours.

So by assigning a Native American to a prestigious guard slot, Clayton's superiors believed they would be giving the lie to Soviet claims of discrimination and lack of opportunity for minorities in the U.S.

How well was Clayton Lonetree prepared for his showcase assignment?

"The (MSG) school at Quantico, Virginia," columnist Otis Pike wrote in the *Dallas Morning News*, "where Marine guards are trained is tougher to get through than Harvard or Princeton. Thirty percent of those who enter get busted out." But not usually for academic reasons, and certainly not for failure to grasp the more sophisticated risks and demands of their elite duty. Much of what gets taught at the MSG school at Quantico involves proper social manners—how to be polite, deferential, how to exercise protocol. In short, how to follow orders and do what you're told. And Clayton had learned that early on, from Baptist school and from his father.

The events that brought Clayton Lonetree to grief began in September 1985, in the last months of his assignment to the U.S. Embassy in Moscow.

2

VIOLETTA

Clayton stood guard at Post Number One, a glassed-in booth at the front door of the embassy. There he began to notice a pretty young woman entering the building daily. She was Violetta Sanni, a Soviet translator who spoke fluent English, and at first Clayton didn't know she was an FSN, a Foreign Service National under regular embassy employment. Certainly she dressed like a Westerner. Lonetree nodded to her each time she entered or left the building, and she began to smile back.

Their first actual meeting came on the Moscow Metro. Since his arrival in Moscow Clayton had wanted to learn what he could about the Soviet Union, expecting that such knowledge could help him later in a diplomatic career, so he had taken to touring the city, scouring out-of-the-way neighborhoods on long subway rides by himself. In addition, he had hired a tutor and started to learn Russian.

Clayton saw Violetta sitting at the end of the car, went over and said, "Hi."

"Why are you here?" she asked in English.

"Just taking a ride."

"It's unusual to see an American on the Moscow subway."

Clayton struggled to make small talk, held back by his bash-fulness and awed by the woman's beauty, but Violetta soon got off the train and Clayton continued to the end of the line.

The question of whether the KGB planned this meeting became an important issue at the court-martial almost two years later. As did, though we were not allowed to pursue the matter, the pos-sibility that a U.S. official helped the Soviets entrap Lonetree.

Their next meeting, a brief one, came at the Marine Corps Ball, held in Spaso House, the American ambassador's official residence in Moscow, on November 8, 1985. Violetta, a guest of the State Department, danced with Clayton once. Other Marines also found her attractive and invited her to dance.

They met again about three weeks after the Marine Ball, again on the Metro. Clayton took a seat beside her and, still fumbling for words, tried to learn more about her. This time Violetta was willing to carry the conversation. She told him she was a Ukrain-ian Jew and talked at length about the Soviet Union. She said she loved her country very much but disliked the government making life for its citizens so restrictive. She mentioned in par-ticular the lack of freedom of movement which kept her from visiting other countries.

This time Clayton got off at Violetta's stop, the second from the last on that Metro line, and together they walked and talked for several blocks. They talked about the Soviet Union and the United States, about music, literature, the arts, people. Violetta expressed interest in fashion and movies. *Gone with the Wind,* she said, was her favorite.

She asked Clayton questions about himself, listened intently to every reply, praised his achievements, and expressed confi-dence that he'd fulfill his dreams of a diplomatic career. They were walking through a low-rent district on the outskirts of the city, and Violetta told Clayton she lived in a small one-bedroom apartment on the fifth floor of a large building with her mother and nine-year-old sister. But well short of her home, she stopped and said she would continue the rest of the way herself. Clayton got the impression she was nervous about being seen with him, that the KGB might be watching them and this could mean trou-ble for her. Although Clayton was wearing civilian clothes, his high-and-tight haircut pointed him out as an American Marine. So they parted, and Clayton returned to the subway and the heart of the city.

With the exception of Nancy Snyder, no woman had ever paid him so much attention. Beautiful, about twenty-six years old, five feet seven inches, with gray eyes, Violetta had made a deep impression on the lonely Marine. She seemed invariably cheerful and happy, full of life (already he had affectionately nicknamed her "Crazy").

The young Native American, twenty-five, the same height as Violetta, couldn't get her out of his mind. But he also knew he was risking his career as a Marine Security Guard if he were spotted with her. A Marine Corps regulation prohibits fraternization with Foreign Service Nationals in nonemployment-related situations in Eastern bloc countries.

This nonfraternization regulation was honored in Moscow mostly in the breach. Clayton knew about the rule, but he also knew that Marine Guards and embassy personnel ignored it routinely. He could recall, for example, how during their initial orientation, Marine Guards were told where prostitutes could be found in the city, and that it was okay to solicit them.

During his own indoctrination, another Marine had asked, "How can you recognize a woman as Soviet, since many speak fluent English?"

"It's easy," the instructing gunnery sergeant answered. "Soviet women have poor-quality shoes and bad breath."

Still, the nonfraternization rule stood officially in the books.

Before Clayton could see Violetta again, he was assigned to temporary duty in Geneva. In Switzerland the young Native American served as a special guard for President Reagan and Secretary of State Shultz at the arms reduction talks.

Violetta dominated Clayton's thoughts during his stay in Geneva. Knowing she liked Western fashion, he bought her a number of glossy magazines, like *Glamour*. Unavailable in Moscow, they would be a welcome present when he returned.

The evening when Clayton walked her part-way home, Violetta had described in detail the building she lived in (hoping he could find it? he wondered). Soon after his return to Moscow, he took

the Metro to her stop and set out, and shortly there it was. The
building contained no elevator, so Clayton walked up the five
floors.

Violetta's little sister answered the door, seemed to realize who
he was, and invited him in. Violetta was there, as was her mother.

The apartment walls were very thin, and after he had presented
his magazines and joined Violetta on a sofa, Clayton heard a couple arguing in the apartment upstairs. He could tell that Violetta's
mother, who didn't speak English, was nervous about having an
American Marine in her home. Clayton assumed she feared that
the KGB had them under surveillance, or that her neighbors
would report him.

As did the Mission children, Violetta's sister took to the young
Marine immediately, sitting on his lap. And Clayton naturally liked
her. He still identified with children, with the problems he knew
they had, and enjoyed showing them kindness and attention. But
realizing he made Violetta's mother edgy, Clayton didn't stay long.

He and Violetta began getting together often. They couldn't go
to restaurants and similar public places because Clayton stood
out with his Indian features and regulation Marine haircut—
clearly a U.S. military embassy employee—and by now he had
come to fear notice as much as he believed she did.

They went to Red Square, visited Lenin's tomb, saw the Krem-
lin, site of so much of the history Clayton had read about, the
magnificent onion-domed cathedrals, the Metropol Hotel, Gorky
Park. They were hiding in a crowd, so to speak, walking and
holding hands, and scared the whole time. Violetta kept saying
she feared the KGB, and Clayton was imagining his career ended
if the wrong person saw him, despite the fraternization he was
aware of among other embassy Marines. They took many long
Metro rides.

During this period—January 1986—Violetta asked Clayton if
he would meet her Uncle Sasha, one of her family favorites. Remembering the nervousness of his reception by her mother, and
considering all the precautions they'd taken to avoid notice, her
suggestion surprised Clayton. He wondered about this Uncle
Sasha.

From his voracious reading, Clayton had become something of
a spy buff. He had devoured everything he could find about

VIOLETTA 27

spying, and was particularly fascinated by the nonfiction of John Barron, which included such books as *KGB Today: The Hidden Hand* and *KGB: The Secret Work of Soviet Agents.*

Barron, a former naval intelligence officer specializing in Soviet affairs, impressed Clayton as an authority possessing key sources within the U.S. intelligence community. Understandably. The dust jacket on one of Barron's KGB books proclaims: "The inner workings along with the ruses and subterfuges employed by the KGB today are revealed through the actual experiences of major characters."

Clayton had come to admire Barron and to believe he had learned a great deal from reading him. And to a point he had. But it was all in the context of book knowledge, not in the daily rough-and-tumble of actual espionage experience. He was like a football player who had read a coaching manual by Vince Lombardi and thought it prepared him to play NFL football. Clayton had spent so much time by himself, fantasizing situations, he had begun not only to imagine a life filled with espionage and intrigue, but actually to employ "counterintelligence techniques" in his rendezvous with Violetta.

For instance, going to meet her he would walk to a Metro station, take the train downtown, get off, stroll into a department store, locate a side exit, and amble back outside to catch a taxi. Then he would ride the cab to another department store, repeat the procedure, and board another Metro to take him to his meeting place with Violetta.

During these maneuvers, he wore a bulky coat, carrying another one underneath. At some "key" moment he would change coats—perhaps in the department store, perhaps in the taxi. On the subway, he held a newspaper or magazine right up to eye level, as if reading it, when actually he was peering over the top to check if he'd been put under surveillance.

Years later when Clayton told me about these antics, I had to sigh. I couldn't imagine anyone more conspicuous than a "disguised" Clayton Lonetree.

Clayton asked Violetta why her uncle wanted to meet him.

"No particular reason. I told him about us, and he's interested in American Indians."

"I don't know, Violetta. Are you sure he's not a KGB agent?"

By now he was so in love with her, the ingenuousness of such a question didn't occur to him.

She laughed. "Sasha asked me if *you* were an intelligence agent. CIA, maybe. No, silly, he's my mother's brother, my uncle, and he's a lawyer. He's not a KGB agent. But if you don't want to meet my family," she said with a pout, "I'll understand."

"No, I'll go meet him. When do you want to go?"

"What about tomorrow?"

She seemed glad that he'd agreed, and kissed him tenderly on the cheek. His suspicion faded. It gave him such pleasure to make her happy, and, after all, she sought very little in return for the joy she provided.

The following day they took a taxi to Sasha's apartment. At Clayton's insistence they got out a few blocks from their destination and walked the rest of the way.

Sasha didn't speak English this first visit, so Violetta translated for him.

Perhaps forty, over six feet tall, elegant and slender, Sasha appeared courtly, scholarly, and quite distinguished to Clayton. Despite the man's drab, baggy clothes, Clayton was impressed, especially by Sasha's clean and tidy apartment. There was a color TV, new drapes, carpets on the floor, freshly painted walls. Nothing fancy, Clayton decided, but very nice.

The host made tea, and through Violetta they talked about Clayton's home and his upbringing. Clayton was less than forthcoming in his responses, more from embarrassment than from any consciousness of security. Sasha inquired about where he'd been, what he did in the States, how he liked his tour in the Soviet Union, and to these questions Clayton had no trouble responding.

Clayton stayed an hour, took Violetta home, and returned to the embassy. The meeting had left him with mixed emotions. He liked this Uncle Sasha, thought him a "nice guy," a gentleman. Yet he had to wonder if there might be more to Sasha's intentions than mere interest in the young Marine's life in America, or getting to know his niece's boyfriend.

At that first meeting, Sasha had registered concern for Violetta if the KGB found out about the romance, and Clayton worried about that too.

But there was something else as well, something born of the young Native American's consummately naive idealism, and his recent absorption with the books of John Barron and "counter-intelligence techniques." If Sasha was a KGB agent, perhaps Clayton could find out something from Sasha. Something that might help ease the differences between the U.S. and the USSR— not so much between their governments and armies, nor between the KGB and the CIA, but between their peoples. Maybe he could change something, do good, "be somebody." So far he had lived an almost invisible life, but in his fantasies, his lonely daydreams, he could stand out like a colossus. As a boy Clayton had drawn swastikas in a school notebook, not as an Indian symbol but out of his fascination with Hitler, the century's most notorious nobody-turned-somebody. While Hitler had been his fascination then, now it was the Soviet Union.

By this time Clayton's Russian had improved to the point where he could visit and talk with villagers in areas at the end of the Metro line. The climate reminded him of his hometown, St. Paul, and the people seemed essentially the same.

He decided to see Sasha again, and to risk his being indeed a KGB agent.

3

SASHA

Up to now in his Moscow adventures, Clayton had violated only the often ignored nonfraternization rule.

Upon his second visit with Sasha, in February 1986, the stakes jumped to another level.

Violetta took him to Sasha's flat, and now there was a dramatic change in the Soviet: he spoke good English, directly to Clayton, without Violetta's translation. Still the father figure, and evidently to explain the transformation, he said he had become greatly concerned with the couple's "extremely dangerous position."

"But," he said to Clayton, "you can help."

"How?"

"Do you know any CIA agents?"

Clayton lied. "No, I don't."

His answer prompted an argument in Russian between Violetta and her uncle. Clayton didn't yet understand the language well enough to follow the rapid, heated conversation, but he assumed Violetta was arguing that it was unlikely they could help their "position" by getting information out of Clayton in return for KGB understanding. Finally she said in English, "Anyway, Sasha, maybe he doesn't know."

Sasha turned to Clayton and said sternly, "Violetta can get out of this, but you can't."

The veiled threat made Clayton wonder if his suspicions weren't being borne out: maybe Sasha was a KGB agent.

The Soviet began asking questions—innocuous questions the Marine could answer readily enough—all the time watching Clayton closely and writing his answers in a notebook. Then he came to something more serious. He wanted plans of the embassy's top-secret floor, including the Crypto Room, heart of the message center.

Clayton stalled, saying he'd have to check. With his mind jumbled, still trying to reconcile the unsmiling Sasha with the benevolent one, he kept telling him and Violetta that he loved his country. He knew he sounded pathetic, though the two Soviets seemed to understand. Or at least so he thought.

But then he caught himself. His mind went back to his notions of using Sasha—to his romanticized spy fantasies, his new-found idealism about Russia and America, his longtime ambition to "be somebody"—and he decided to become a double agent, to play along with Sasha and gather as much information as possible before reporting the situation to American intelligence.

Which is what he ultimately did . . . though grossly underestimating the people he dealt with on both sides.

After that second meeting with Sasha, Clayton and Violetta went to her apartment—now with her mother and sister conveniently absent—and made love. It never occurred to Clayton—starry-eyed, attention-starved, blinded by love—that Violetta had entrapped him. Even when I was questioning him a year later, when he finally realized the gravity of facing court-martial for espionage, Clayton couldn't bring himself to believe that his Russian lover had betrayed him.

During the rest of his Moscow tour, about two months, they had the opportunity to make love three times, and even then it was hurry up before mother and sister return, and hush up because neighbors might hear.

One time, just after they had made love, Clayton turned to Violetta and, because he liked to tease her, said, "You're a KGB agent, aren't you?"

"I don't think that's funny," she said.

"But you are," Clayton prodded.

"I'm not. But you may be CIA."

"What a stupid broad."

Whereupon she slapped him. Ever passive, Clayton didn't re-taliate. Violetta ordered him out of the flat, so Clayton meekly put on his clothes and returned to the embassy, wondering why he'd been risking himself. But the next day, back he came. Violetta scolded him for being late.

Clayton's next meeting with Sasha was scheduled for late Feb-ruary. For some time Clayton had known, without telling Violetta or Sasha, that on March 10 he would be transferred to embassy duty in Vienna. On the one hand he was glad for this chance to put distance between himself and the Moscow situation, but on the other he was afraid to break off with Sasha and risk being turned in. He decided he would stall for time, telling Violetta of his transfer but withholding the news from Sasha until their meeting.

To play along with Violetta's uncle, Clayton brought to their third meeting the embassy "floor plan" Sasha had requested. Ac-tually, it was a fire escape schematic similar to the notices posted near the embassy elevators. The diagram, unclassified, was easily obtained by anyone with embassy access.

Sasha seemed satisfied. He then showed Clayton photographs of men who worked at the embassy, and other photos of their wives, and asked him which men were intelligence agents. Clay-ton said he didn't know if any of them were, but to string the Soviet along he pointed out that Sasha had mismatched some of the wives and husbands. Sasha had the photos laid out on the dining room table, and Clayton moved the pictures around to pair the actual couples.

"Why don't you know if they're intelligence agents?" Sasha asked. "Don't you work with them?"

"Yes, but they don't wear signs. Agents all have a cover."

"Maybe you don't know they're agents, but I do. And I know there are others I'm not aware of. I want to find out who they are. I want their pictures before you leave Moscow."

Clayton, convinced that Sasha did know who the intelligence

agents were, eventually gave the Soviet photos of three people he suspected were agents, two of whom had already left Moscow.

Whatever that compliance was worth, Clayton rationalized it as a matter of staying in Sasha's good graces. But another opportunity presented itself at that third meeting that could more directly serve Clayton's notions of using his situation to operate as a double agent. Sasha had spoken of a KGB general who went by the name of "George," supposedly a member of the Soviet Central Committee. When Sasha said there might be a chance for Clayton to meet George in Vienna, Clayton responded with enthusiasm.

The last topic of the meeting was Violetta. When Clayton had advised Violetta of his transfer to Vienna, he told her that she should date others while he was away and that he would do the same. Violetta had said she wouldn't allow it. (That she couldn't control him never occurred to Clayton, and he gave me a puzzled look whenever I pointed this out.) Now Clayton told Sasha that he thought it unfair for Violetta not to see other men after he left Moscow. Sasha appeared shocked, and solemnly he made Clayton promise not to hurt Violetta by seeing other women.

Sasha suggested, "After you leave Moscow, telephone Violetta only once. And don't write to her. That could implicate her for the KGB." Acting the concerned uncle, he offered to deliver letters between Moscow and Vienna.

Told of Violetta's enthusiasm for the plan, Clayton agreed.

"Since you're leaving the country in a few days," Sasha warned, "I don't think we should meet again in Moscow." He spread out a map of Vienna and pointed to an intersection. "The Vienna Opera House is here. I'll meet you there in early summer." Bringing the meeting to a close, he told Clayton, as he had before, "When you come back to Moscow, you can have a flat, a car, *and* your relationship with Violetta."

The young Indian understood Sasha's offer, but he had no intention of defecting.

Clayton used accrued leave time for a Frankfurt stopover before reporting for duty at the Vienna embassy in mid-March. His non-duty life in Germany alternated between reading newly purchased spy books and getting drunk. The spy books, even novels, might give him ideas on how to cope with his problem, he'd decided, and the alcohol allowed him to forget it—to forget everything, in fact. Several times, not used to heavy drinking, he blacked out and couldn't remember what he'd done or where he'd been.

Clayton found the atmosphere in Vienna more relaxed than in Moscow, but he thought the people generally rather "snobbish." Still, he loved the beauty of the city, its restaurants and opera house; he studied Vienna's history and took German lessons. And he became acquainted with a young Austrian named Jan Augustin, and Augustin's girlfriend. They were part of a heavy-drinking set, and both would eventually be brought to America to testify at Clayton's court-martial.

Some of the other Marine Guards in Vienna took to calling Clayton "Running Bear," because each day he put on combat boots and ran five miles up the mountain behind the barracks. He loved running, now that his father no longer ran ahead calling, "Come on, girls."

Clayton had agreed to meet Sasha at the Vienna Opera House in June, on a Sunday evening. "Sasha's favorite time," Violetta had told him. Still hoping to use Sasha as a line to valuable Soviet information, Clayton kept the appointment and found the Russian waiting.

Sasha's animated handshaking and hugging on the crowded street embarrassed Clayton. The avuncular Sasha told Clayton he looked troubled and thin. "Don't worry. Everything will be okay," Sasha said. "Violetta sends best regards. The next time we meet, I'll bring a letter from her."

Why hadn't he brought one this time? Clayton wondered. He loved his beautiful Violetta and believed she loved him; whoever this "Uncle Sasha" was and whatever he was up to, Violetta he still wholeheartedly trusted.

Sasha took Clayton out to dinner that night, put his arm around him, and said, "You're going to be part of my family."

At a subsequent dinner Clayton suggested that Sasha buy new clothes, some that matched, because he stood out in Vienna, looked too much like a Soviet. Perhaps taking this bit of comradely advice as a sign of Clayton's need for friendship, Sasha began to ingratiate himself with the impressionable Native American. He confided that he had a fiancée. And once, in a park, as they sat by the edge of a pond, Sasha told him all about fish: the kind of schools they travel in, and how to catch them. It worked. Clayton would remember their relationship in Vienna as that between a father and son.

"I knew Sash really liked me," Clayton was to tell me.

On another afternoon they strolled through the picturesque Vienna Woods, enjoying the tranquillity of one of Europe's most lovely spots. Sasha told Clayton he reminded him of Violetta, who also loved the outdoors. That's when Sasha said he'd come back in the fall. The Marine had been telling Sasha that after this visit, it would be best they not meet again, but now, with his new feeling for Sasha reinforcing his adoration of Violetta, Clayton agreed to see the Soviet when he returned to Vienna. He'd already gone this far, enjoying Sasha's attentions and hoping to obtain information from him or the shadowy "George." Having long decided to reveal all his clandestine activities with the Soviets to his Marine superiors, he saw no reason to quit now. He wanted his efforts to produce something worthwhile. Why, he might even come out looking good. A somebody.

Of course, Clayton was completely overmatched in his little espionage game with Sasha, as should have become clear even to this most naive of "spies" when, at a lunch one day, Sasha laid a thousand dollars in Austrian currency on the table. "A present."

"I can't take the money."

"If you don't, you're insulting me."

They argued, Sasha appearing perplexed and deeply offended. "You're insulting me and our relationship," he said.

How could Clayton not believe him? How could he hurt the feelings of the fatherly Sasha? Sasha might be a KGB agent, but to Clayton he was also a friend, a kindly older man who cared for him.

Clayton let the money lie a long time, trying to sort out his emotions. Finally he took it, having cleared his conscience with a decision on what to do with the money: he went to a store and bought a dress for Violetta and Western shirts and ties for Sasha. His actual bill came to more than a thousand dollars.

Two other times Clayton took money from Sasha—a total of twenty-five hundred dollars—and on these occasions Sasha insisted that the money be for Clayton himself.

"I want you to have a good time," Sasha assured the young Native American, adding that he'd be "hurt" if Clayton didn't enjoy the gifts. So Clayton did, almost as if obeying an order. The Marine eventually blew it on drinks for himself and bar-hopping buddies, soaking up the Vienna night life.

He rationalized that this was not personally benefitting from the money. Throwing it away in bars gave pleasure to others and couldn't be counted as his own material gain. Besides, since he fully intended to reveal his activities with Sasha to the appropriate authorities when the time was right, his having gone so far as to establish exchange of money could count in his favor toward his ability to continue as a double agent.

Sasha said he would return to Vienna in late September. Clayton, by now realizing that his going along with Sasha might amount to digging his own grave, put in for leave for the first part of the month. Maybe, he thought, he could clear his head before his next encounter with Sasha.

He went to Munich, stayed at the Marine House, and got drunk. He went to Stockholm, stayed at the Marine House, and got drunk. In Finland he did the same thing. The oblivion of booze helped blur the big problems he faced. The clearheadedness he'd looked forward to, the few times he was sober, only scared the daylights out of him.

Sasha didn't show up as scheduled, and Clayton again found himself torn by conflicting emotions. He had heard about a terrible ferryboat accident in the Black Sea, and part of him hoped that Sasha had been aboard and had perished; another part chastised such a death wish for his "friend."

Not to worry. Sasha arrived in early October, meeting Clayton outside a church, explaining his lateness by saying "personal business" had kept him in Moscow. He wore a big grin and hugged the Native American. "How are you, my friend? Good to see you. I missed you."

They had a long conversation about Moscow, and Sasha asked Clayton if he knew Edward Lee Howard, a CIA agent who had defected to Moscow. "I met Howard and I like him," Sasha said. "He wants his wife and family brought to Moscow, and it is being arranged." Sasha said the KGB, very pleased with the American defector's identification of CIA agents and their Moscow contacts, had scheduled him for a speaking tour of the Soviet Union. Sasha described Howard's roomy apartment, color TV, car, and a farm the government had set aside for when his family would come over. Clayton realized that Sasha was painting a picture of *his* life should he defect. It was a rare instance when Lonetree had it right.

They talked about Nicholas Daniloff, the *U.S. News & World Report* correspondent arrested in Moscow as a spy.

"I don't like Russia's taking a journalist," Clayton said, "because that does nothing for the good of either country. Just the opposite. It promotes unrest between the nations."

"The U.S. did the same thing to a Soviet in New York, Gennadi Zakharov."

"I'd hope the Soviets were above that stuff."

"I hope we all are."

Sasha brought pictures from Violetta, along with letters asking several times when Clayton intended to come back. She had made Sasha promise to ask about Clayton's plans for returning to Moscow because she missed him "terribly."

Still deeply in love with Violetta but not wanting to open the Moscow can of worms, Clayton changed the subject by telling Sasha about a language school he was attending in Vienna. Sasha observed it would be a good idea if he went "to Monterey."

Monterey. The reference was to the top-secret intelligence language school located in Monterey, California. By now so muddled was his thinking Lonetree didn't recognize the significance of Sasha's knowing about its existence, while on his side the Soviet agent seemed to enjoy playing his little games with the Marine—like the time he had talked about "catching fish."

Over dinner one night, Sasha announced that because of failing health he would soon have to stop traveling from Moscow to Vienna. Perhaps one more visit, and then Clayton would meet and work with the KGB officer named George.

Finally beginning to appreciate the damaging information

Sasha had on him, Clayton decided he needed "health insurance" and concocted a far-fetched scheme to create incriminating evidence against Sasha. He approached a woman he later described as a cocktail waitress and offered her a hundred dollars to meet Sasha in a park—a meeting Clayton would arrange—and to entice him into a compromising sexual scene that Clayton could photograph from nearby and use to get the Soviet off his back.

Clayton scheduled a meeting for himself with Sasha, then hid in some bushes near the rendezvous point with his camera.

Alas, Sasha arrived only to wait and wait. The woman didn't show. (Clayton found out later she'd mixed up the directions and gone to another part of the park.) When it became obvious she wouldn't appear, Clayton hopped out of the bushes and kept his own appointment.

Clayton didn't see Sasha again through October and all of November. He returned to his drinking and, after one horrendous bout, ended up in Alcoholics Anonymous.

It happened in early October. Clayton and a friend drank a bottle and a half of vodka and became rowdy. The next day Clayton couldn't remember anything. His gunnery sergeant referred him to a doctor for medical evaluation of his drinking problem, and a Dr. Rigamer sent him to an English-language A.A. group in Vienna. But Clayton went only a few times, and no superior questioned him when he stopped attending.

Clayton saw Sasha the first week of December, intending it to be their last meeting. He felt he couldn't go on. Having played along with the Russian for so long preyed on his mind, and he had come to despair of obtaining valuable information from the Soviet to justify what he had done. They met at a church and Sasha took him to dinner. At the restaurant they were joined by George.

For months Clayton had dreamed about this meeting, at first eager for the opportunity, but more lately dreading it. Sasha introduced George as a KGB general and, fantastically for almost anyone else but Clayton, as a member of the Soviet Central Committee. The Native American could still believe that such a superluminary might have a genuine interest in him.

But this man was no father figure. George's eyes were cold and humorless, and with his piercing stare he glared at Sasha as chillingly as at Clayton.

About fifty, five feet eleven inches with a medium build, George appeared to be in rock-hard shape, and he dressed better than Sasha, not so conspicuously Russian. He had gray hair and "weird" gray eyes. "Cold-blooded" came immediately to Clayton's mind, like a stereotypical KGB agent described in John Barron's books. George spoke softly and politely, but totally without humor. Clayton didn't remember him smiling even once. Months later, talking to me, he still sounded afraid of George.

George went to the phone, was gone a few minutes, came back, said he had to leave, and told Clayton he would meet him December 26 at St. Wenceslaus Church at seven P.M. He gave the Marine a piece of paper with the directions, said goodbye, and left.

Then Sasha said he had to leave too. As they shook hands that last time, Sasha said, "Whatever you do, don't play with this person," then he turned and walked away. It was the last time Clayton saw him.

The Marine guard decided, probably correctly, that the meeting "transferred" him from Sasha to George. He also judged, and here he turned out to be wrong, that George ranked above Sasha.

Anticipating the December meeting with George, Clayton expected to receive detailed instructions he wouldn't be able to bring himself to follow—delivery of top-secret material. He had the distinct impression George would be very different from Sasha, and that either he'd have to deliver or be exposed, or even killed.

As it happened, Clayton accidentally found himself in a position to fulfill George's wildest expectations, but he didn't act on it. And with that decision, he also realized that his plan to operate as a double agent—still his justifying hope—needed help. Unable to deal with the terrifying George alone, he made up his mind to go to America's own intelligence agency.

It happened a few nights after his meeting with George at the restaurant. Assigned to embassy roving patrol—making rounds to check offices for security violations such as exposed classified documents or unlocked desk drawers—Clayton entered the chargé d'affaires's office and found the safe door open.

According to regulations, when an MSG on roving patrol discovered such a security violation, he was to (1) conduct a cursory search of the safe to determine if the contents had been disturbed; (2) check the classification of those contents; (3) secure the safe; and (4) write a report.

This report—much like a traffic ticket, listing date, time, and location of offense—was to be made out in triplicate: one copy got left on the desk of the offending office occupant; one copy went to the RSO (Regional Service Officer); and one copy went to the Marine Detachment Commander.

Clayton found this open safe in the office of the embassy's second-in-command, a man outranked only by the ambassador. Clayton's first thought was: "There's enough stuff here to keep George and Sasha happy for a long time."

He had to examine the contents to determine the category of classified information. The degree of the offense in a security violation depends on the classification of the material exposed. Clayton found envelopes stamped TOP SECRET and six small envelopes he knew contained combinations to all the remaining safes in the embassy.

He recalled how excited Sasha had been when he'd given him those useless floor plans and outdated pictures. Here he was facing the real thing: top-secret documents from the chargé d'affaires's office, plus access to all other safes in the U.S. Embassy in Vienna. Clayton could simply open those unsealed envelopes, Xerox the contents, replace the envelopes, and repeat the procedure at the other safes. He was in a position to turn over to the Soviet Union literally *all* the secrets of the U.S. Embassy. No one would know. Nothing would be missing.

Clayton slammed the safe door shut and wrote up the offense. So disturbed he could hardly control his hand, he completed the slip and walked into the hallway, closing the office door behind him. Soaked with sweat despite the chill pervading the embassy at night, he wobbled weak and scared to the first chair available in the corridor, sat down heavily, clenched his eyes closed. He desperately wanted to throw his head back and get his breathing to return to normal, but the ornately carved high back of the chair wouldn't permit it. He leaned forward, hanging his head. His breathing finally regained a semblance of normal rhythm instead of the painful panting precipitated by finding the open safe.

"God, what's happening to me?" he said aloud. Head hanging limply, Clayton opened his eyes. He had his dress blue hat in his lap and his gaze fell on the insignia: the anchor, globe, and eagle. Never having known such depression, caused by that split-second moment when he'd thought of how delighted George and Sasha would be to receive his information, the sight of the Corps insignia came as an emotional slap in the face to the Native American sergeant.

"You almost did it this time," a part of him said aloud, the voice bouncing down the deserted corridor.

"What are you going to do?" another part of him asked.

"I can't go on like this, I just can't," the first voice lamented. "What *should* I do?"

"End it!" The voice, not unlike his own, spoke in a command tone.

Clayton twisted in the ornate chair, half expecting to see someone standing behind him, maybe one of his gunnery sergeants. But no one shared the corridor with him; he was still alone in the embassy hallway.

However, in the sudden turn to seek a source for his own voice, he heard the solid thump of his .38 calibre revolver striking the heavy wood arm of the chair.

"There's your solution," advised Voice Two.

Clayton withdrew the fully loaded .38 from its shiny black holster and cradled it almost dreamily beside the Marine Corps insignia on his hat. "You're right," said Voice Number One. "The only way is to end it. No more Sasha or George, or, for that matter, Violetta. Oh, you love her, all right, but it can't work. It never could. It will be a blessed relief not to face this whole thing any more."

Clayton sat and stared at the weapon and the insignia, unaware of the passing time, plunged in remorse. Perhaps killing himself would restore some of his family's dignity. Hadn't his grandfather spoken of honor and dignity a long time ago?

"Do it."

He raised the revolver and his head at the same time. Staring straight ahead, seeing nothing in the dim light of the shadowy hall, he gently placed the muzzle of the weapon under his chin. He felt a twinge as the front sight dug into the soft tissue beneath his jaw.

Clayton eased the hammer back, hearing and feeling two sharp clicks as it cocked into firing position. Carefully he inserted his right finger into the trigger guard, trembling, just a pound-and-a-half squeeze from oblivion, hardly more than the touch of a feather.

"Do it!"

"Yes."

"God damn it, do it!"

"Okay."

"Damn you, do it!"

"No! That won't get it, Sergeant, no way," he heard with surprising clarity.

Drenched with sweat, Clayton realized in a sudden moment of truth that suicide would end the nightmare only for himself, and would let down all those people to whom he had obligations: the Marine Corps, especially the Marine guards; his parents and his brother; the revered Mitchell Red Cloud.

Poised with the cocked pistol under his chin, the thought of Red Cloud filled his head just before he lowered the weapon.

Desultorily continuing his rounds at the embassy, weaving and wobbling on weakened legs, he searched in his mind for a way out. And decided that he needed help.

Clayton had been in Vienna for ten months and knew the identities of the American "spooks." He even had a good idea who headed the U.S. intelligence operation, and resolved to contact the man.

A few days later—at the annual Embassy Party at the ambassador's residence, on December 14—Clayton had a few drinks, then walked into the ballroom and introduced himself to Harold Johnson [not the man's real name]. Sasha had pegged Johnson as the CIA chief of station in Vienna, but Clayton would have figured this was his man simply on the basis of his own embassy experience.

"Oh, yes," Johnson said. "I've seen you around. What can I do for you?"

"I have some serious problems, sir. I need to talk to you."

"What sort of problems?"

"It concerns my tour of duty at our Moscow embassy, sir. While I was there, I had unreported contacts with Soviets."

Johnson looked around, as if noticing the roomful of people for the first time. He placed his drink on a small table, put his hand on Clayton's arm, and said, "Let's go into the hall."

Out in the corridor adjacent to the ballroom, Johnson said, "This is a serious matter. Tell me a couple of things. Who did you meet in Moscow?"

"I met a man named Sasha. I think he's a KGB agent."

"Did you report it?"

"No, sir."

"Was there a woman involved?"

"No, sir." Clayton was lying to protect Violetta, whose involvement he still believed to be either unwilling or coincidental. He waited for Johnson to respond. The suspense made his fingertips tingle. It had taken him a long time to screw up the courage to come forward.

Johnson shrugged, glanced over his shoulder at some other guests, and said in a semiwhisper, "Well, Sergeant, we're at a party; this isn't any place to discuss the matter. Call me in the morning at my office and we'll get together."

"What time should I call, sir?"

"Nine o'clock."

"Thank you, sir. I will."

4

"SORT OF LIKE YOUR PARTNER"

Clayton felt relieved; he had set the process in motion. Every day, in Moscow and Vienna, he'd worried that his meetings would be discovered and his career end in shame, but now at last he wouldn't have to carry the burden himself; he was plugging into the official apparatus.

Clayton telephoned the next morning at nine using the name "Sam," as Johnson had instructed, and the CIA station chief said to meet him at the McDonald's in the center of Vienna that afternoon.

Johnson was sitting at a table outside. Clayton arrived fifteen minutes late, having gone through his full repertoire of counter-intelligence safeguards: the newspaper-in-front-of-the-face trick, and Metro to department store to taxi to Metro transportation.

Finally he walked up to Johnson and said in the crisp tones of a seasoned operator, "Sorry I'm late, sir. Christmas traffic, you know."

Johnson stood up and shook his hand. Clayton thought, *He's using some kind of signal,* and began looking up to rooftops and at parked cars for people in trench coats. Johnson was wearing a trench coat, and other guards at the embassy had joked that only spooks wore them: Want to know how many agents are at an embassy? Count the trench coats.

As he looked around, Clayton noticed a young man seated on the opposite side of the outdoor restaurant, drinking coffee and, sure enough, wearing a trench coat. *He can't be one of them,* Clayton thought. *He's too young.*

"Sit down, Sergeant, don't be nervous," Johnson said. "As you probably know, I'm in charge of this station. I asked one of my men, Charles Trunk [not his real name], our counterintelligence agent, to come with me today. He'll debrief you."

"Yes, sir. Where is he?"

Johnson pointed out the young man in the trench coat.

"Don't let his apparent youth fool you. He's our leading counterintelligence agent in Europe, and he'll be working with you. Sort of like your partner."

If Clayton hadn't been so caught up in his counterespionage fantasy, he could have, at this point, used the advantage of his tremendous bargaining position and asked for immunity—they'd have given anything to hear his story—but with Johnson himself playing out the fantasy, Clayton missed his opportunity.

"Come on, I'll introduce you to your new partner," Johnson said. They joined the other trench coat.

"Charlie, this is Sergeant Lonetree, the MSG at the embassy I told you about last night. Sergeant Lonetree, I'd like you to meet Charles R. Trunk, my best agent. I hope you two can resolve our little problem to the company's advantage."

"Call me Charlie," Trunk said, motioning the Marine to sit down, "and I'll call you Clay."

Johnson told them to take it from there and good luck. He left.

Trunk looked like an Ivy Leaguer just graduated from Harvard Business School, young and clean-cut.

They talked for a few minutes in general terms about Clayton's activities in Vienna and Moscow, nothing about Sasha, Violetta, or George. Trunk then said, "Do you know the location of the Intercontinental Hotel?"

"Yes, it's a very prominent hotel in the heart of Vienna."

"Meet me there between three-thirty and four. I'll have a room. I want to hear your story to determine our next move." Trunk paused a moment, looking from side to side. "In thirty seconds I'm going to get up and leave. Stay here. Wait five minutes, then leave. I don't care what you do between now and then, but be sure to meet me at the Intercontinental's lobby bar. Try not to be followed. Any questions?"

"No, sir. I'll be there."

Trunk got up and walked away. Clayton, convinced he was living a real-life spy drama, stayed the prescribed five minutes, trying to ascertain if anyone was watching him. Who knew, the rooftops could be crawling with KGB agents.

Clayton killed the next couple of hours before his appointment playing the role of sightseer and window-shopper. Though this was something he normally enjoyed, he couldn't really get into it because he saw agents—friendly or otherwise, he couldn't tell—in every reflection and shadow. Clayton wondered if he'd become paranoid.

Trunk was sitting at a corner table in the Intercontinental bar when Clayton walked over and shook hands. "Here I am, Charlie."

Trunk smiled. "Glad to see you, Clay. Sit down. Have a drink."

"No thanks." He wanted to keep a clear head, but his mouth was so dry he needed something, so he ordered a ginger ale.

After Clayton had finished his drink, they went to the room Trunk had rented "to talk." The agent said he wouldn't tape the meeting, but asked if he could take notes. Of course, the compliant Marine agreed.

Although no tapes of that conversation were introduced in evidence, it's hard to believe it was not recorded. Trunk's hotel room featured all the technical equipment of an MGM sound stage, unseen by Lonetree.

Once settled in the room, the agent said he wanted to hear Clayton's story and wouldn't interrupt much.

"Where should I start?"

"At the beginning. When you got to Moscow."

Clayton told him everything, including Sasha's offer of a flat and a car in Moscow, how Sasha said the Soviet Union would consider him a friend, even the money he'd received. He advised Trunk about his relationship with Violetta, and with her mother and sister.

The friendly Trunk took notes and listened.

Clayton mentioned his interest in language and tutoring in Moscow and Vienna, listening to Moscow radio stations, trying to read Russian books and newspapers, and visiting the countryside to meet ordinary Russians. They also talked about Lonetree being a double agent, and about trying to get Edward Lee Howard out of the Soviet Union. Trunk exhibited special interest in the planned meeting at the church with George. He showed the Marine several dated pictures, all of them of young men, and Clayton finally settled on one that looked to be an earlier photo of George.

When did Clayton finally realize that the government had no intention of using him as a double agent? Incredibly, not until his court-martial was almost over.

Just as significant, neither Johnson nor Trunk read Clayton his Miranda rights—that is, their equivalent under the Military Code of Justice, Article 31. The Marine sergeant continued to believe he was being interviewed for a job, when in reality he was incriminating himself.

Clayton told Trunk he thought he could contact Howard in Moscow through Sasha. Trunk, although seeming enthusiastic, remained noncommittal, repeating that his superiors would have to make the decision. (Actually, Lonetree's plan was being considered seriously by the CIA during the time of his meetings with Trunk. For almost two weeks secret cables were being exchanged between Vienna and CIA headquarters in Langley, Virginia, until it was decided that sending the young Marine after Howard was too risky, given the possibility that Lonetree, clearly still in love with Violetta, would be tempted to defect.)

As this first meeting ended, Trunk told Clayton to resume his regular schedule at the embassy, and not to tell anyone they were talking, especially Clayton's detachment commander or the RSO.

Why? Because had Clayton talked to someone else, he might well have been given an Article 31 warning and told to see an attorney. Trunk flat out told Lonetree *not* to seek advice, to "trust me."

Clayton stood guard for over a week and saw Trunk three additional times, rescheduling a couple of the meetings around his guard duty. They discussed the possibility of Clayton becoming a double agent, and the upcoming meeting with George.

Trunk scheduled their next and, as it turned out, last meeting for Christmas Eve, at the Intercontinental Hotel. But this time they would not be alone. Trunk said some government agents, "also assigned to counterintelligence," wanted to meet Clayton.

When I and the other members of Clayton's defense team learned of the CIA involvement, it didn't take special legal expertise to envision the major struggle ahead of us: having Lonetree's statements to the new agents, personnel of the Naval Investigative Service (NIS), ruled inadmissible because everything he told them had first been given to the CIA (who passed the information along to NIS), and was obtained in violation of the UCMJ, specifically Article 31, requiring that a suspect be read his rights.

On December 14, 1986, when the young Marine had approached Johnson at the Christmas party, he had volunteered information sufficient to communicate to any trained and competent agent that he had engaged in contacts with Warsaw Pact nationals in violation of the published nonfraternization policy of the State Department and the Marine Corps. We were also certain that the information Lonetree subsequently provided should have shown to any trained agent that Lonetree was in over his head, needed help, and had been solicited to engage in espionage through a sequence of unlawful meetings and activities.

Instead of acknowledging this, Johnson and Trunk had tantalized Lonetree, continually whetting his appetite for double-agent duty, appreciating that the Native American had been bouncing the idea around in his head almost from the beginning of the affair. Clearly, Trunk and Johnson had taken advantage of Lonetree's respect for their authority, all the while acting as conduits for the criminal investigation that would culminate in his own court-martial.

If the court were to suppress Lonetree's statements, the military would have no case. No "investigation" was responsible for catching this alleged "superspy." In fact, *they didn't catch him; he came forward.* Everything the prosecutors knew came from the defendant himself.

Still, while any such legal redress might save our client, it didn't matter nearly as much as seeing justice done. Lonetree's "crimes," fully recounted here, weighed little against a system that put a troubled, inexperienced, trusting youth into the position to commit them. The young Marine, his mind swimming in a tangle of espionage reading, young love, and delusions of outwitting the KGB, had done nothing more than use bad judgment, had committed no actual crime other than fraternization, and transmitted two pieces of innocuous information.

And for this the government sought the death penalty.

It didn't make sense. Something larger had to be lurking behind the major status accorded this minor Marine.

Clayton had no idea why Trunk was turning him over to another agency, and to the Naval Investigative Service at that.

A largely civilian service arm, the NIS had traditionally devoted most of its efforts to investigating such petty allegations as theft, AWOLs and suspected homosexuality. Whenever it did get a major case, such as the John Walker spy investigation, it bungled it badly. Writing on the Lonetree case in the *Washington Post* on February 7, 1988, Pete Earley summed up the agency's reputation: "Within the intelligence community, the Naval Investigative Service had long been regarded with disdain . . . Whenever a major crime was committed, the FBI was called in. The NIS's track record has been so poor that in 1985, legislation was introduced in Congress to abolish it."

How the NIS was placed in charge of the Lonetree case, and was then encouraged to engineer the grotesque "Moscow spy scandal" that grew out of it, is a question that can be answered only by the highest echelons of the State Department and the Department of Defense, probably more the latter. What now seems all too clear, however, is that this gang-that-couldn't-investigate-straight seized on the young Native American as a most juicy opportunity to redeem its record in the eyes of the intelligence community by showing him up to be the Marine Corps' first genuine master spy.

Of course Clayton himself had no idea that his new keepers were indeed agents of the NIS. In the Intercontinental coffee shop, Charles Trunk simply said, "Sergeant Lonetree, I want you to meet these guys, some of my colleagues in counterintelligence."

There were three of them at the coffee-shop table. Somebody said, "Let's sit down," and everybody but Trunk did. Trunk said, "Sergeant Lonetree, I'm going to leave you with these men. Try to help them with what they want."

Clayton and the new agents didn't stay long in the Intercontinental coffee shop. One of them said, "Let's go to our hotel, get some sandwiches, and talk in the room. Is that okay with you?"

"Sure," Clayton said. "Whatever you want."

They went to the Strudelhof Hotel, located in downtown Vienna, a short taxi ride from the Intercontinental. The agent who seemed in charge ordered sandwiches and coffee from room service and told Clayton to relax. This man, David Moyer, showed Clayton his identification and had him sign some Article 31 (Miranda) warnings. He asked if Clayton understood what he'd signed, and Clayton said yes.

But he didn't know *why* he'd had to sign them. He thought he was working *with* these men, that these were ordinary procedures spies and counterspies went through and that his signing the papers was necessary to his continuing to work with them.

Nor did he understand that he had been set up. Johnson had sought and received information from Clayton about the "classic vulnerabilities, drugs, alcohol, sex, and money." After being told no classified material had been conveyed to the Soviets, Johnson arranged the first of several meetings with Trunk—a CIA colleague and specialist in counterintelligence. Trunk, in turn, decided it was important to obtain counterintelligence information as fast as possible from Lonetree by inducing him to continue his disclosures. He told Lonetree that such disclosures would be "confidential," that it couldn't possibly harm him to be forthcoming and truthful; in short, it couldn't hurt him to cooperate. "Sort of like your partner," was how Johnson had described Trunk.

Some partner! He partnered Clayton straight to facing the death penalty.

But he acted like a partner. Trunk seemed happy to discuss Lonetree's possible participation as a double agent, something the young spy buff dearly desired. Until finally, with everything already known, Trunk turned the Marine over to the prosecuting arm of the NIS.

The first thing Moyer asked Clayton after he'd signed the Article 31 papers at the Strudelhof was whether he would mind going to their London headquarters for debriefing. Clayton said, "I just got through doing that with Trunk."

Moyer insisted that it was important. But he didn't say *why* Clayton had to go through it all again—that all the information to date had been illegally obtained because he hadn't been given his rights.

Even though Clayton didn't understand, he figured he'd better go along. He told Moyer that traveling to London would be okay but he'd have to get his clothes from the Marine House. Moyer said, "No, we'll leave from here." He instructed one of the others, Agent Hardgrove, to make reservations for three on the first flight out to Heathrow. He also arranged for Lonetree's gear to be brought over from the Marine House, thus ensuring that Clayton wouldn't run into a friendly Marine who might give him some badly needed advice.

On and off for the next four days at the Holiday Inn near Heathrow Airport, they hammered away at Clayton. On the third day they brought in a man named Brannon.

"Tell us more, tell us more," Clayton remembered Brannon saying.

"There is no more."

"Then make something up. Lie to us."

Lonetree, ever eager to please, did just that. He made up some whoppers.

Finally, frustrated and exhausted, Clayton clammed up. He simply had no more to say. He had told the NIS everything he knew, even lied to them when asked to lie, and still the agents kept telling him to keep going. There wasn't anything to keep going about. Maybe, he thought, these people were not friends, as he'd been led to believe. He would wait until Trunk's people, or Trunk himself, came back into the picture.

On New Year's Eve, Clayton and James Austin, an "expert on Soviet affairs," flew back to the United States. Lonetree, still not aware of what faced him, asked what qualifications he'd need as a double agent.

"You'll have to talk to somebody else about that," Austin replied.

Two unsmiling men in civilian clothes met them at the Washington National Airport gate. They took Clayton to a waiting staff car for the forty-mile ride south to Quantico.

Clayton sat in the back seat that cold night, the two men in the front. Several times he asked questions about the duties of a double agent, but was greeted with stony silence. He shrugged off the rudeness. Obviously someone else would brief him on his assignment.

The only communication in the car came as they neared the base. "Helluva way to spend New Year's Eve, isn't it?" the driver said to his partner.

They drove past the monument depicting the Marines planting the United States flag at Iwo Jima. One of them had been a Pima Indian, Ira Hays, and a warmth spread inside Clayton. He felt as if he'd arrived back home. He had attended MSG school here. He was sure something much bigger awaited him now.

That it wasn't to be training or assignment as a double agent still didn't dawn on him when they brought him to the brig and he heard one of them say, "Book him for espionage." He thought even this was part of the act.

A few days after being settled into a five-by-nine foot cell, no inmates allowed nearby, Clayton took stock of his situation and decided it might not be all bad. This could be a test to determine his toughness. More likely, the CIA had other Machiavellian reasons for letting him be locked up. The young Native American thought hard about his situation.

Early on he received his jailhouse orientation: "Don't talk to anyone. Not inmates. Not guards. Not anybody. You'll be held in solitary confinement, locked down. You'll be kept in isolation at all times. You'll eat your meals in your cell. This is done for your own safety which, frankly, I personally am not concerned about. You've disgraced the Marine Corps."

With plenty of time to think and fantasize, and unable to grip the reality of his situation, Clayton imagined the CIA masterminding a spectacular jailbreak, spiriting him out of the country and setting him to work on bringing Edward Lee Howard back to America.

The actual scenario, he finally decided, would be more prosaic. Someone, probably Trunk, would march into the brig with the proper papers, put his arm around him, and walk him right out of there. Those hostile guards would see him in a different light then. And of course he'd hold nothing against them.

Counterspy and double agent were titles that thrilled Clayton, and in elaborate detail he pictured the moment when Trunk would give him the assignment.

"Sergeant Lonetree. Clay, I mean. Your code name is Lone Wolf. But first things first. We've got a lot to talk about. Don't be afraid to interrupt. I'll want your total input. What the Company wants you to do is . . ."

Clayton had no access to TV or radio, and the occasional newspaper he received had everything related to himself cut out. It was just as well. Not knowing what went on helped strengthen daydreams of rescue, which in turn made the abuse he received endurable.

"You're a traitor, Cochise," one guard told him. "You've dishonored the Marine Corps, and you'll find there's not a single Marine, not one, who doesn't hate you."

And, "Here's your chow, Dead Man."

And, "Haven't they killed you yet, Indian?"

Some Marines, apparently out of kindness, said nothing.

They let him outside when nobody was around, and happy for the chance to get some exercise, Clayton tried to get in some running. It wasn't easy. He was wearing leg irons, a belly chain, and handcuffs. When I learned this story I had to think of the man his fellow Marines had called Running Bear.

Not much happened in Quantico for the next few months. Except for the omnipresent guards, Clayton didn't see anybody, didn't talk to anybody, remained alone with his thoughts of intervention and salvation from outside. He put up a picture of a farm scene on his cell wall as a reminder of the outdoors, but a guard took it down.

Clayton still expected release at any moment. Meanwhile, Secretary of Defense Caspar Weinberger, questioned during a press conference several weeks after the arrest, said, "He should be hung, but I guess these days we just shoot them."

PART TWO

Article 32

5

THE GREEN ROOM

The whole incredible case started for the defense with a phone call from Sally Tsosie to my old friend, Las Vegas attorney Michael Stuhff.

It figured that Sally would reach out to Mike. A Catholic seminary student and 1973 University of Utah graduate, Mike had decided upon finishing school to devote a year to helping Sally's hard-pressed people on the expansive Navajo reservation. But instead of one year Mike stayed thirteen, earning little money but lots of friends in places like Fort Defiance and Window Rock.

The January 20, 1987, message to call Sally marked the first time Stuhff had heard from her since 1985, when he moved from the reservation to private practice in Las Vegas. He had represented Sally and her mother Louise Benally in a long and heated Navajo-Hopi land dispute initiated by a hastily drafted executive order in 1882 and perpetuated for a century by governmental bungling and wrangling.

Stuhff waited until he got home to answer Sally's call, expecting a relaxed conversation with her to catch up on the latest news from Big Mountain. An actively committed Native American very different from the confused teenager who gave birth to Clayton in Chicago in 1961, Sally was a five-foot-two-inch dynamo who always knew exactly what went on in the Navajo's neverending fight with the government.

Stuhff had told me of his respect for his friend's abundantly admirable qualities: honesty, forthrightness, a deep concern for her people, bravery, determination and, not paradoxically, a pervasive gentleness. She grew up on the reservation in the Big Mountain area before moving to Chicago as an adolescent and later taught Navajo language to young Indian schoolchildren.

Stuhff had no idea why Sally phoned, but he looked forward to talking with her. They had ridden out some rough times and celebrated a few victories together. She had been with Mike on one of the land-dispute cases while picketers had brandished protest signs inside the courtroom. Other times he'd had to shout over beating drums and Navajo songs outside the courtroom.

"Hello, Sally. How's it going? Haven't heard from you for a long time."

"Mr. Stuhff, you've got to help me." Sally was trying to maintain a calm, steady voice, but Stuhff could tell right away that there was a problem.

"What's the matter?"

"Remember my son Clayton . . . went into the Marine Security Guard Program?"

"Of course, I remember."

"He's in trouble."

Mike could feel Sally's concern over the phone. Other mothers might have reached a hysterical pitch by now in a similar situation, but Sally was holding a steady course. As was typical of Navajos from the lawyer's experience. They radiated enormous spiritual strength.

"What kind of trouble?"

"He's being court-martialed."

"Why?"

"He guarded the embassies in Moscow and Vienna. He's charged with espionage."

Stuhff was no expert on military law, but he knew espionage carried a maximum sentence of execution. He couldn't believe that Clayton would be involved in any such major crime, an illusion Sally quickly shattered.

"They're talking death penalty." Sally's voice finally cracked.

"Where's Clayton being held?"

"At the brig in Quantico, Virginia. At the Marine base. He's in solitary confinement. No one will tell me anything."

Mike had learned Navajos do not cry. But Sally Tsosie sounded very close.

"How did this happen?"

"No one will answer my questions. I'm his mother and they won't talk to me. They only say he was involved with this woman."

"Who's *they*?"

"The Marines. A Marine defense attorney. Major Henderson."

"Henderson represents Clayton?"

"The Marines appointed him. I can't really find out anything."

"Sally, this is very serious. Clayton needs a lawyer who's not a part of the military."

"I know. That's why I called you."

Stuhff tried to get his bearings. He and I had just worked the Judge Harry E. Claiborne impeachment, the first impeachment to go before the U.S. Senate in fifty years, and there was also a murder case he'd recently taken all the way to the U.S. Supreme Court, which had granted a new hearing. Both cases, done *pro bono,* had left him drained financially as well as emotionally. The thirty-seven-year-old lawyer, married and with four children, had never made much money, a situation he'd been hoping to remedy by establishing private practice in his native Nevada. He hated to turn down his friend Sally and her husband, a member of the Navajo Tribal Council, whom he also admired.

His first thought was that an eastern lawyer, someone closer to the scene, could better serve Clayton's needs. A major espionage case promised long hours and little pay, and he expected that his wife Sandra, who was teaching kindergarten to help make ends meet, would prefer he stay away from it, though on the other hand he knew she wouldn't complain if he got involved.

"Sally, why don't you call a friend of mine in New York, Michael Kennedy. He just finished an espionage case, *In Re Koecher,* and did a hell of a job. Michael is one of the brightest, hardest-working lawyers in the country. He really understands, and he's not afraid. If I faced an espionage charge, he's the man I'd want."

"What's his phone number?"

"I don't have it with me; I'm at home. But you can get it from New York City directory assistance. Call him. Say I recommended him. Then call me. And if you can't get hold of him, I'll call him tomorrow. I want to make sure a competent lawyer takes care of you and Clayton."

The next morning, I walked into Mike's office in the Valley Bank Building on Fourth Street and said, "Let's go to the Horseshoe for ham and eggs." I considered their two-dollar breakfast, with a ham slice bigger than the plate holding it, the best value in the county.

"In a minute. First, I've got to call Michael Kennedy in New York. Stick around if you want to say hello."

"I do indeed." Kennedy and I were old friends. "Why are you calling Michael?"

"I'm referring a case to him."

"Oh?" A private investigator needs to be curious.

"You remember Sally Tsosie. Her son is in the Marines. He was guarding the U.S. Embassy in Moscow."

"Right."

"Clayton's facing a general court-martial for espionage. They say he got mixed up with a woman over there. Now he's accused of giving secrets to the Soviets."

"Why do you want to pass the case to Kennedy?" I had my own long history of working with Indians, and every time I had felt better after doing it. Actually, my history with Navajos stretched back farther than Mike's. I'd headed the investigative team defending the two-thousand-plus felony charges that arose out of the 1973 seventy-two-day occupation of Wounded Knee on the Pine Ridge Reservation in South Dakota. And for years I taught classes to the Indians, training tribal members in the fundamentals of legal investigations. It seemed to me Mike and I should be in on this case.

"Kennedy just did an espionage. Defending Clayton could cost a hunk, in time and money. I don't know anything about military law. I . . ."

"You guys went to the same schools, didn't you? Took the same courses, right? What does Kennedy know that you don't?"

"A lot. He's got experience."

"Hell, Mike, you're a good lawyer. Catching up on military law isn't that tough. Besides"—I smiled—"you've got a leading expert right here, in the flesh."

He laughed. "That's right. You worked that fragging case."

A young black G.I., Billy Dean Smith, had been court-martialed for murder, accused of throwing a grenade into an officer's tent in Vietnam. My investigation helped win an acquittal in a seemingly hopeless case the army brass had made clear they expected to win. The court-martial panel—the military equivalent of a civilian jury—consisted of six combat veterans, two of whom had themselves been fragged.

"Mike," I said, "courts-martial aren't much different from regular criminal trials."

"It's financial."

"I think we can raise money. You've got a member of an oppressed minority here. Just like Big Mountain. Or Wounded Knee."

My optimism didn't impress Stuhff. He hadn't gotten rich on Big Mountain, and he knew I'd dipped into my own pocket to help pay expenses at Wounded Knee. For Mike, "raise some money" translated into not having to hock furniture to finish a case. Throughout his career he had handled cases *pro bono*, increasingly wondering if his efforts made a difference, if they really helped. I harbored no doubts that they did, but my view might be a matter of perspective: my three sons were grown and on their own.

But Mike and I had gone off on crusades before, and I felt that an important case involving a Navajo rightly belonged to us. Realizing that my attempt to make the financially strapped Stuhff feel like a money-grubbing mercenary wasn't working, I tried a different tack.

"Think about the publicity. Everybody will be watching this one."

Stuhff considered this an even weaker argument. True, the Lonetree case could attract additional business, but it would most likely be the free kind worked for principle. Victories won for Indians and other oppressed groups usually did not impress better-off clients, i.e., those able to pay.

"I don't know, Lake. I just don't feel up to this one."

"Damnit, Mike, let's take a shot. Sally needs help. She's a friend and deserves the kind of personal attention we'll give her."

I knew Stuhff would do it. And sure enough, instead of phoning Mike Kennedy, he shortly called Sally Tsosie in Tuba City, Arizona, and told her he would represent her son. In turn, she told him she'd just learned that Clayton's father, Spencer Lonetree, had contacted William Kunstler.

Stuhff felt an immediate wave of relief. He knew that Kunstler would do a good job. Stuhff had admired the famous attorney for years, and one time he had heard him speak at the University of Utah Law School.

He remembered that occasion well, having met Kunstler personally in the student lounge after his talk. Mike's wife Sandy had brought their three-and-a-half-year-old son Paul, whom Kunstler entertained with jokes and games while Stuhff envisioned reminding Paul one day of how he'd met the crusading lawyer.

Mike recalled his conversation with Kunstler. A law student who'd studied five years for the priesthood at St. Joseph's College in Mountain View, California, Mike had suggested Nuremberg-type trials for General Westmoreland and President Nixon. Kunstler responded, "You are far too radical." Stuhff had thought it ironic that Kunstler termed *him* a radical, especially since his fellow students at the conservative university considered him a "square."

Stuhff's good feelings about not having to handle the Lonetree case were short-lived. When he called Kunstler in New York to congratulate him, Kunstler said, "I'm not representing Clayton."

"Why not?"

"I talked to him on the phone," Kunstler explained. "He said, 'Can you hold a minute? I need to talk to somebody here.' When he came back on the line, he said, 'I don't want a civilian lawyer, or any publicity. I'll send you a letter about why I don't need your help.' "

(The letter, dated January 21, 1987, and hand-printed in ink, arrived in due course and read: "Dear Mr. Kunstler: Sir, I believe it's appropriate to inform you by this letter that I have reached the decision to decline your services, however it's nothing against you. I feel it's in my best interest to go through this very discreetly and as much as possible. But I do appreciate your services. That was kind of you. Thank you. Sincerely, Clayton Lonetree, Sgt., USMC.)"

Kunstler's news dismayed both Stuhff and me. From a cursory check of the press stories, we knew Lonetree's trial would be a major political event. It seemed strange, to say the least, that someone in Clayton's position would not want to have independent counsel from a civilian, from a lawyer not subject to military control. Either Lonetree was too trusting and naive, thinking he could avoid adverse publicity (although no one then could have imagined the worldwide attention the case actually received), or he'd been persuaded by others at Quantico to turn down Kunstler's offer.

Clayton's mother had no such illusions. Sally didn't trust the military to give her son a fair trial, and worse, she didn't think her son understood what he faced. After further conversations with Kunstler and Stuhff, she retained Mike and me to represent her son, hoping to change Clayton's mind about civilian counsel.

Sally succeeded, and on January 31, 1987, Mike and I arrived at National Airport in Washington, D.C., rented a car, and drove forty miles south to check into the Quality Inn directly across the street from the entrance to Quantico Marine Base.

Before leaving the motel to meet Marine Capt. Andy Strotman, a military lawyer who had promised to show us unclassified NIS files—at this point we couldn't review classified material—I secured our room so that I'd be able to tell if someone had broken in during our absence. My experience in a good many controversial cases, including the murder of Phoenix, Arizona reporter Don Bolles (a case in which my investigative work helped clear two men unjustly convicted of the crime and secured their release from Death Row), had taught me the value of such caution.

The four-inch-thick file Strotman passed on to us at Quantico kept us awake most of the night. Reading NIS's account of Clayton's background and activities in Moscow and Vienna, we immediately realized the defense's major problem: Sgt. Clayton Lonetree had confessed. Transcripts of his detailed statements to NIS agents, all tape-recorded, filled more than two hundred and fifty almost marginless and closely spaced pages.

That we knew confessions obtained during lengthy, isolated interrogations are often unreliable, exaggerated, and falsely incriminating gave small comfort. Confessions are extremely hard to beat.

During this first visit of ours to Quantico, the confessions themselves were classified as secret, and thus not for our eyes. When we finally were able to review the actual confessions, we found evidence of wholesale manipulation, abuse, and "shaping" of Lonetree's statements by the agents who had interrogated him. These agents had extracted "admissions" that Clayton had stolen and delivered top secret documents *which their own subsequent investigation determined did not even exist.*

Reading Lonetree's service record, I began to get a picture of Clayton Lonetree—a young enlisted Marine conditioned to respond unquestioningly to authority figures—as a textbook subject for such manipulation. His own superiors had evaluated Lonetree in Moscow. In polite, bureaucratic prose they described him as a Marine sergeant who "ardently strives to produce acceptable results and is frequently successful in this regard." Malleable, easily impressed, dominated by authority (and I still hadn't learned of Clayton's disturbed childhood), he stood out as naive and eager to please. When we eventually learned the extent of his "confessions," we knew therein lay the key not only to his prosecution but to his defense.

With less than two hours sleep, Stuhff and I met the next morning, Sunday, with one of Lonetree's military attorneys, Maj. David Henderson. I liked him immediately. About forty, with a wry sense of humor, Henderson had "two more years but who's counting" to retirement.

A slender five feet eleven inches, he appeared in good shape from daily workouts. The major had two fingertips missing, a result of his cabinet-making hobby. ("My doctor says I'm mad at my left hand.")

Henderson had grown up in Oklahoma, married a Louisiana Cajun, and had three children. He spoke softly and with pride about them and his colonial-style house. The Marine Corps had paid his scholarship to law school.

Over breakfast in a diner near our motel, I got the impression Henderson genuinely wanted to help Lonetree. Nevertheless I decided to adopt a wait-and-see attitude as to how far this Marine officer would go in risking his career for a noncom charged with the emotionally loaded crime of espionage.

Henderson, with his considerable head start on Mike and me, was well versed in the case, and he exhibited special expertise on procedural intricacies of military law. He believed the only hope for the defense was a speedy trial motion. He didn't think the prosecution could put together a strong enough case in the ninety days normally allowed by the Uniform Code of Military Justice.

Stuhff and I disagreed. Unusual cases can extend and/or suspend the speedy trial requirements of the UCMJ, and the Lonetree case certainly qualified as unusual. More important, we realized, the Marine Corps, the Justice Department, Department of Defense, CIA, and NIS could devote unlimited resources and manpower to this case. (Eventually, their joint task force detailed to the Lonetree investigation, codenamed "Cabin Boy," would total more than one hundred government investigators and forty lawyers.)

We went along with Major Henderson "for the time being." However, we needed to learn more before committing to a court-martial date less than ninety days away.

Henderson, Stuhff, and I visited Clayton in the Marine brig on February 1, Stuhff and I for the first time, in a depressing institutional green room. We sat on black Naugahyde chairs under fluorescent lighting. Barred windows in this model penal facility framed a bleak view of barren trees outside the cinder-block structure we had entered through electronic gates. A Marine guard periodically peered through a barred opening in the door, and I assumed the room was monitored electronically.

Clayton, wearing camouflage fatigues and a yellow plastic badge bearing his name and photograph, hardly resembled the stereotypical rough-and-ready Marine. He stood five feet seven inches, looked very slight at 135 pounds, had straight black hair cut "high and tight," prominent cheekbones, and dark sensitive eyes. There was no denying he looked like an Indian. He seemed grateful at the arrival of people working on his behalf, and right at the start of the meeting he confirmed that he wanted Mike and me to represent him.

I was struck immediately by Clayton's frailness, particularly his delicate hands, which appeared more suited to playing a piano than manning an M–16. He appeared unfrightened and exhibited extreme politeness—"Sir," "Mr. Headley," "Mr. Stuhff," "Major Henderson." A likable kid. Very shy, almost stoic, eager to please. And not entirely resigned to a bad fate, I was to learn. For even then, Clayton was still clinging to the hope that the CIA would accept his double-agent offer.

For Stuhff and me, the room was all too familiar. A few months before we had sat here, in the same chairs, talking to our client, Judge Harry E. Claiborne, being held at the Quantico brig during his impeachment proceedings. We'd been talking about Judge Claiborne today as we drove through the gates to Quantico, passing the famous Iwo Jima monument commemorating the February 23, 1945, raising of the American flag on Mount Surabachi.

Stuhff emphasized to Clayton that we'd do everything we could to help. He and I had agreed that a great injustice was in the making, and we wanted to assure this most vulnerable youngster that we would see to it that everything possible would be done for him.

I questioned Clayton for a long time that first day. He answered everything in a quietly straightforward manner, leaving me with the overwhelming impression of a naive, lonely G.I. who'd been trapped (but by whom?) into a love affair that had gained him little and the Soviets less. Certainly he was no hardened traitor. Remarkably, under the circumstances, he kept professing a deep love for the U.S. and the Marine Corps and the government that wanted to execute him.

But more important to me than Clayton's feelings about his accusers was the question of what he'd actually *done*. I couldn't yet begin to understand why so many higher-ups wanted his head.

6

KUNSTLER FOR THE DEFENSE

I rang the doorbell of a brownstone comfortably nestled on Gay Street in Greenwich Village. It was early afternoon, February 2, and Stuhff and I had to wait barely a minute before being admitted. Down a few steps in a basement office waiting room we found William Kunstler standing near a seated woman. She looked familiar.

"Joey," Kunstler said, "these people have come a long way. You'll have to wait."

Of course, I thought, she's Joey Heatherton.

"Okay," the actress said cheerfully enough before Kunstler had to inform her that his business with Mike and me would require her return another day.

Kunstler maintained a small, efficient office, packed with law books and memorabilia from past cases. A working lawyer's office, not decorated to impress. Old brick and old wood.

"I like your place," Stuhff said.

"It's been in my family a long time." Kunstler stood more than six feet tall, with bushy sideburns. Characteristically, he was wearing his glasses on top of his balding head. Polite, gentlemanly, not at all the fanatic fire-breather of right-wing caricature.

But then this was not my first time with Bill Kunstler. As soon as we were inside his office, he said, "Lake," and gave me a hug. "It's good to see you again." Then, turning to Stuhff, "Lake and I were at Wounded Knee together."

"I see you've got a peace pipe from Wounded Knee," I said.

"Yes. Leonard Crow Dog gave that to me." A Sioux medicine man, Crow Dog enjoyed tremendous prestige among Native American peoples.

Kunstler apparently wanted to reminisce about our exhilarating days defending the Indians who occupied Wounded Knee. "Have you seen Carter Camp lately?" he asked.

"He's stayed with me a number of times," I answered. Carter Camp, the Ponca Indian and former head of the American Indian Movement (AIM) and the Warrior Society, a brave, intelligent man, had been an early organizer for Cesar Chavez.

"How about Stan Holder?"

The Oklahoma Indian was the second most decorated soldier in Vietnam, where he had served three tours. Later he denounced the war and personally set up the defense for the besieged Indians at Wounded Knee.

"Holder is still active," I said, "but I haven't seen him."

"What about Russ Means?"

"I talk with him once in a while. And I see a lot of Dennis Banks."

Banks's wife had recently given birth to their thirteenth child, the first boy after twelve girls. I smiled recalling Banks and Means: Means, under Carter Camp's leadership, aided in the occupation of the Bureau of Indian Affairs (BIA) building in Washington, D.C.

Mementos of Kunstler's remarkable career filled his office: B.A. from Yale, law degree from Columbia; World War II hero; teacher at Columbia, New York University, Pace College, and the New School for Social Research.

Books he had authored filled his shelves, not only works dealing with his wide-ranging law career—including *First Degree* (1961), *The Minister and the Choir Singer* (1964), *The Hall-Mills Murder Case* (1981)—but also collections of his poetry and essays. A Phi

Beta Kappa, Kunstler had published in the *Columbia Law Review,*
the *Yale Law Review,* virtually every major magazine and newspaper in the country. Here and there were photographs, letters,
and other documents of the cases that had established his reputation: *Hobson* v. *Hansen,* the landmark civil rights case; *Mis-
sissippi* v. *Thomas,* the famous 1961 Freedom Rider case; his
representation of David Dellinger in the Chicago Eight conspiracy
case, of Adam Clayton Powell, Jr., in his reinstatement to Congress; of Martin Luther King, Jr., as special trial counsel; of Daniel
Berrigan, accused of destroying draft records in Catonsville,
Maryland; and, more recently, of Leonard Peltier, wrongly convicted for the murder of two FBI agents on the Pine Ridge Indian
Reservation in South Dakota.

Anyone standing in that office, whatever his politics, would
have had to recognize that William Kunstler, almost seventy years
old, virtually embodied the civil rights movement in the United
States.

That afternoon, however, Kunstler seemed more intent on get-
ting out of his office than on staying to continue our discussion.
He had two daughters by his second marriage to Margaret L.
Ratner, possessor of a doctorate of jurisprudence degree from Co-
lumbia, and presently Stuhff and I found ourselves accompanying
Kunstler through Greenwich Village toward the Little Red
Schoolhouse to pick up the younger girl, age eight.

Kunstler walked fast. Though by now intent on the Lonetree
case, he paused to point out St. Josephs' Church, which decades
ago headquartered the Catholic Worker Movement and was frequented by Dorothy Day.

I'd forgotten how much I liked New York City, especially
Greenwich Village, a small town set down in the midst of a dynamic, bustling metropolis. It was a special experience to see it
in Kunstler's company. We couldn't progress far without someone
stopping to greet him.

"We'd really like you with us on this case," Stuhff said.

"Michael, I know how Clayton feels. He's very G.I. My reputation frightens him."

"Lonetree thinks he can avoid publicity. He thinks it all will just go away if he keeps quiet. But we know that's impossible. You read the papers. The administration wants to kill him. I hope you'll come back on the case."

Stuhff did indeed want Kunstler's experience and expertise and, yes, the honor of working with him. But he had another motive, too. Financially exhausted from the Claiborne impeachment trial, he would need money and organization to defend Clayton Lonetree. Kunstler could raise money, and he certainly had the organization—the Center for Constitutional Rights.

"Does Clayton want me on the case?"

"We had a long conversation with him yesterday," Stuhff said. "He knows I represented his mother, and that she trusts me. We showed him some of the press. He's beginning to see the seriousness of his situation and that he's going to make headlines, like it or not. We told him a good defense would require a major cooperative effort, and we briefed him on your work. When we see him tomorrow, I want to tell him you're available."

We walked a little further in silence.

"Clayton has to realize," Kunstler said, "that he's a scapegoat for other problems. Iran-Contra, possibly. God knows what else. The three of us know how they'll use him. I have no idea who he conferred with at the brig during our phone conversation, but a lot of people don't want this looked at. They'd like to sweep it under the rug: let him plead guilty and pretend all their problems are over. It's easier to do that to a minority member. Read the newspapers. Watch TV. It doesn't take special insight to see what's happening."

I shared Kunstler's view. The government was finding itself in the uncomfortable position of saying that a lone Indian noncom belonged in the same category as the legendary Kim Philby, the British intelligence official who for years had supplied secrets to the Soviets.

We'd already had indication, I told Kunstler, that the authorities intended to play hardball. After talking with Lonetree the day before, Stuhff and I had returned to our motel room and found it unmade. I called the front desk and was told a DO NOT DISTURB sign had been hung from the doorknob. Stuhff or I hadn't done it, but before either of us could draw breath to deny hanging the sign, the motel manager blurted: "The maid finally looked in anyway, and one of you told her, 'I'm gonna be sleeping, and so is my friend in the other room.' "

Immediately upon hanging up the phone I checked my suitcase. I always align its zipper in an exact manner to detect tampering. The zipper was in a different position. We filed a protest over the incident the next morning, before driving up to see Kunstler. (Another such incident occurred shortly afterward. Stuhff and I, driving a rental car, found ourselves tailed by a green-and-white military police vehicle. Our complaint wound up with Frank Petersen, a three-star general and commanding officer of Quantico, who was quoted as saying, "I'm not worried about the lawyers. It's that investigator.")

Kunstler wasn't any more surprised by the entry of our motel room than we had been, yet it seemed to have its effect.

"Can you be at the Article 32?" Stuhff asked Kunstler flat out.

The Article 32 hearing, set to begin Wednesday, February 4, was more or less comparable to a grand jury or preliminary hearing in civilian law, though different in two respects: unlike the grand jury because the defense could have its say, and unlike a preliminary hearing because there was no skilled prosecutor to sidestep evidence he didn't want introduced. The military's Article 32 gave us an advantage provided by no civilian counterpart: we could challenge the basic premise of the case—whether the prosecution possessed sufficient evidence to warrant a court-martial.

Still, the lion's mouth awaited, and with precious little preparation time.

"Lake and I," Stuhff continued, "have already read hundreds of pages of unclassified material. But it's just that—unclassified. We have to obtain clearances for the classified documents. And no matter, we need your help."

"I'll be there," Kunstler said casually, making our trip to New York a success, but then added, "if Clayton wants me."

"We're headed back to Quantico this evening. Tomorrow we'll tell Clayton you're available."

Stuhff wheeled our rented Ford Taurus through National Airport the next day, February 3, to pick up Kunstler, flying in from

New York. The two lawyers talked about similarities between KGB and CIA practices, Stuhff recalling a 1979 incident in which two undercover KGB officers entered an Indian bar in Flagstaff, Arizona, and got in an argument with a Navajo Marine veteran over which weapon—the American M–16 or the Russian AK–47—ranked superior. Standard KGB, according to the FBI agents who interviewed Stuhff afterwards. Soviet agents regularly land on the West Coast, said the FBI, and like any businessmen on a junket routinely visit Disneyland, then the Grand Canyon, often using Flagstaff as a watering hole in between—followed all the way by American agents. And, according to Stuhff's FBI interrogators, the CIA operates similarly in the Soviet Union, where KGB counterintelligence agents have just as easy a time determining the Americans' movements. Neither of the two great powers' intelligence agencies seemed to have the monopoly on drunks and Maxwell Smart screw-ups.

Clayton had readily agreed to Kunstler as a defense counsel, which somewhat surprised me. Now Kunstler surprised Stuhff and me by saying, "Mike, you should be lead counsel."

Stuhff thought this over. Lead counsel with Kunstler on the team? The remarkable and generous offer was like a pro football mastermind coach, say George Halas, telling a second-year quarterback to call his own plays.

"I have these other cases for the Center," Kunstler said, "and I've heard good things about you from my friends in Arizona. If you can take the burden of organizing it, I'll give you all the help I can."

"I ran up a lot of debts working on Claiborne and can't afford to finance another crusade. I've handled the kinds of cases that pay to fund this apparent hobby of mine, but I just haven't had enough of them."

"I know what you mean," Kunstler said. "I remember doing the desegregation case for the D.C. school districts. I was all by myself and Judge Skelly Wright told me a major organization should handle it. I came into the courtroom every day with my heart in my throat, wondering if I could survive another twenty-four hours. But we should be able to raise something on this one, Michael. I'll do what I can."

Later, on our way out of Hockmuth Hall, site of the Article 32 hearing, we noticed a display case of service medals, from the Congressional Medal on down.

I pointed out the Legion of Merit. "My father got that," I said proudly.

Kunstler said, pointing to the Bronze Star, "I have that one." Then he pointed to the Purple Heart. "And four of those."

7

CLEARANCES

February 4, 1987
1339 HOURS

"The hearing will come to order," announced Investigating Officer Maj. Robert J. Nourie, uttering the first of many hundreds of thousands of words of what was to become a near-epic legal battle.

Major Nourie, serving as a magistrate without legal authority, would submit recommendations to Quantico Commanding General Petersen at the end of the Article 32 pretrial investigation. Petersen would then have to decide whether to press charges against Clayton at a formal court-martial. The defense hoped to make the court-martial unnecessary by showing that the prosecution had no case.

"The purpose of this investigation," Nourie explained, "is to inquire into the truth and form of the charges sworn against Sergeant Clayton J. Lonetree, United States Marine Corps. Copies of these charges—and the order appointing this investigation—have been provided to the accused, counsel for the accused, counsel for the United States, and reporter. Sergeant Lonetree, have you seen these charges against you?"

"Yes, sir," Clayton answered, "I have."

The young Marine faced five charges:

CHARGE ONE

That Clayton "conspired with Violetta Sanni, Aleksiy
G. Yefimov, AKA Uncle Sasha, and Yuriy V. Lysov,
AKA George, to (1) gather names and photographs of
covert agents, (2) plan and conduct meetings in Moscow and Vienna, and (3) secrete in his room a list of
covert agents." Also espionage: "Sergeant Lonetree did
gather information regarding floor plans and office assignments for the Embassies of the United States in
Moscow, USSR, and Vienna, Austria, and did plan and
conduct meetings in Moscow and Vienna with Violetta
Sanni, Aleksiy G. Yefimov, and Yuriy V. Lysov."

CHARGE TWO

"Sergeant Clayton J. Lonetree did, at the United States
Embassy, Moscow, USSR, on or about 10 March 1986,
fail to obey a lawful general order, to wit: paragraph
5–3, Chapter 5, OPNAVINST 5510.1G, dated 20 April
1984, by wrongfully failing to report telephonic, mail
and personal contacts with Violetta Sanni and Aleksiy
G. Yefimov, AKA Uncle Sasha, citizens of a communist
controlled country." Also, "Sergeant Clayton J. Lonetree did, at Vienna, Austria, during November 1986,
violate a lawful general regulation, to wit: Article
1116.2, U.S. Navy Regulations, dated 26 February,
1973, by wrongfully identifying by name covert United
States intelligence agents to Aleksiy G. Yefimov, AKA
Uncle Sasha, a citizen of a communist controlled
country, such information being of possible assistance
to a foreign power."

CHARGE THREE

"Sergeant Clayton J. Lonetree did, at the United States
Embassy, Moscow, USSR, during February 1986, steal
the floor plans to the seventh floor of the said embassy,

of some value, the property of the United States Government. Sergeant Clayton J. Lonetree did, at the United States Embassy, Vienna, Austria, between June and July 1986, steal three photographs, of some value, the property of the United States Government. Sergeant Clayton J. Lonetree did, at the United States Embassy, Vienna, Austria, during November 1986, steal the floor plans of said embassy, of some value, the property of the United States Government."

CHARGE FOUR

Chiefly allegations that Clayton discussed national defense information with Violetta, Sasha, and George.

CHARGE FIVE

"Sergeant Clayton Lonetree did, in Moscow, USSR, and Vienna, Austria, during the period September 1985 to December 1986, with intent or reason to believe that it would be used to the injury of the United States or to the advantage of the Soviet Union, a foreign nation, communicate descriptions of the floor plans and office assignments to the Embassies of the United States in Moscow, USSR, and Vienna, Austria, such information being related to the national defense, to Aleksiy G. Yefimov, AKA Uncle Sasha, a citizen and agent of a foreign government."

The defense intended to show that the actual events did not merit such serious and sinister-sounding charges.

The Article 32 investigation was conducted in a virtually bare, concrete-walled, windowless room in the basement of Hockmuth Hall. No reporters were allowed in the drab enclosure, though many, eager for information, waited outside the building; after all, Defense and State Department officials had said the disclosures in the Lonetree case indicated "serious damage" to national security. But the government would conduct this hearing in guarded secrecy.

Whatever majesty of the law might have been expected for such a capital case stood nowhere in evidence. Investigating Officer Nourie sat behind a plain table at the front of the stark, gray room. Seated behind another such bare table, located directly across the room and to the left of Nourie, were Government Counsel (Prosecutor) Maj. Frank Short, and Assistant Government Prosecutor Capt. J. A. Powell, both of the Marine Corps.

Directly across the room facing Major Nourie on his right sat the accused, Clayton Lonetree, his two military counsels—Maj. David Henderson and Capt. Andy Strotman—and William Kunstler, Mike Stuhff, and myself.

Posted both inside and outside the two doors leading into the room stood spit-shined, eyes-front Marine guards.

Investigating Officer Nourie tried to get the hearing off to a brisk start, but soon tripped up. "By whom do you wish to be defended in this case?" Nourie asked Lonetree.

"By all of them, sir," Clayton said nervously.

"*Them* being lead counsel, Mr. Michael Stuhff, assistant counsel, Mr. William Kunstler, Major Henderson and Captain Strotman?"

"Yes, sir."

"You are advised you have the right to cross-examine the witnesses produced against you at this hearing. Does government counsel have, at this time, a list of prospective witnesses they intend to call?"

"Mr. Investigating Officer," said Prosecutor Short, "at this point the government anticipates calling the following witnesses: Special Agent David Moyer, Special Agent Michael Bruggeman, Gunnery Sergeant Darrell J. Enderlin, and Sergeant E. W. Scott."

Just a minute! A passel of witness was about to be called, and much of the alleged evidence against Lonetree still remained classified.

"One of the problems we've had in this case," Stuhff rose to point out, "is our being denied access to evidence. Therefore I believe it's not proper for the Article 32 to proceed at this point, until we've been provided with the material."

A simple-enough request: the defense wanted to know what it faced.

The issue boiled down to the prosecution having access to evidence the defense did not. Lacking security clearances, the defense stood as firmly chained and handcuffed as Clayton Lonetree when allowed into the yard for exercise.

Nevertheless, Major Nourie, probably under pressure from higher-ups, and Prosecutor Short, clearly raring to have at the accused, wanted to proceed. And proceeding, the defense was convinced, would lead to travesty.

How *could* it go forward?

Kunstler, eloquent and persuasive, addressed the critical issue. Mixing common sense, the Constitution, and simple fair play, Kunstler argued that the defense needed to know what it was defending against. But few people in that secret hearing seemed to hear his words. Certainly Major Nourie remained unimpressed.

Nourie declared that he wanted to proceed. But how could Lonetree's defense go ahead if it didn't know what it faced? Already in this first hour, I was wondering what the press would make of such a farce.

Maj. David Henderson, for the defense, pointed out that "the entire information contained in Sergeant Lonetree's confessions is classified as secret. Even his place of birth and where he went to high school are classified as secret. This is sloppy work, simply classifying the entire document as secret."

The argument raged and tempers grew short. The government wanted the civilian defense team to fill out a personal history form, several pages in length, to establish its security clearance. And while the government considered the decision to grant such clearances, the hearing would proceed! Besides violating Lonetree's constitutional rights, I suspected, and so advised Stuhff and Kunstler, that the detailed information we were being asked to supply might lead to an investigation into *our* pasts. On the other hand, perhaps not: the government already had thick files on all three of us.

Finally it was agreed that the defense team would provide only their names, dates, places of birth, and Social Security numbers for purposes of obtaining security clearances. Nourie optimistically predicted that the clearances would be available the next day.

But it wasn't settled yet. "Does the government desire to go ahead today?" Nourie asked Short.

Short hesitated. What if Lonetree's rights *were* being violated by their proceeding with a shackled defense team?

"The government recommends," Short said, "that prior to going forward, the investigating officer consult with independent legal counsel, and possibly a recess for that purpose would be appropriate. However," he added, "the government is prepared to proceed today."

So even Short wanted to wait! But, as quickly became evident, Major Nourie did not.

"We will proceed at this time," Nourie said. "I assume government counsel is prepared to indicate those areas where we have a problem with security clearance."

Short himself hadn't expected this. "Sir, my first scheduled witness will not testify at all unless all parties present in the hearing room have clearances. Beyond that, I am not sure what areas may be disclosed that are considered classified."

"So we're not speaking solely of physical evidence," Nourie said, "but also testimony?"

"Yes, sir. When I said the government is ready to proceed— my witnesses are here and my evidence is marked—that doesn't mean I'm prepared to go ahead without civilian counsel obtaining clearances."

Finally Nourie saw the light. With the defense opposed to starting, and the prosecution hesitant, he recessed the hearing to the next day. Surely by then the clearance question would be settled.

8

A MUFFLED DEFENSE

February 5, 1987
1339 *HOURS*

With the granting of Limited Access Authority (LAA) still pending, Major Nourie called the Article 32 pretrial investigation to order.

Present were Major Short and Captain Powell for the prosecution, and Major Henderson and Captain Strotman, along with Sergeant Lonetree, for the defense. Kunstler, Stuhff, and I—our clearances unsettled—were absent.

Nourie asked Prosecutor Short about the status of the clearances. Short said he expected an answer this day—check that, the next morning at the latest.

Major Short said, "Mr. Investigating Officer, Rule of Court-Martial 405 Delta–2 Charlie provides that an Article 32 investigation shall not be unduly delayed to allow the presence of civilian counsel at such investigation. I point out for the record that the government is operating under a demand for speedy trial. A witness has been produced for this hearing from London, England, and the defense has been aware of this fact and been given the opportunity to interview the witness. They were aware of it yesterday afternoon when civilian counsel departed."

The "speedy trial" Short referred to was the UCMJ mandate that Lonetree be brought to court-martial within ninety days of his arrest. Henderson believed (Stuhff, Kunstler, and I were dubious, but had registered no protest) that the ninety-day requirement operated in Lonetree's favor, making it more difficult for the prosecution to get its act together.

But wouldn't it also be more difficult for the defense, especially an undermanned defense?

We had decided after the first session not to participate without clearances. There was no way we could represent Clayton without access to the evidence against him. Our decision, endorsed by Clayton (he would agree with all our decisions, trusting us as completely as, earlier, he had put faith in NIS), had little to do with the ninety-day provision. None of us actually believed the government would let the law detour its rush to judgment.

But the government's stampede did give us one advantage: with the prosecution proceeding, the defense, especially myself, gained time to obtain information about the witnesses, data for Stuhff and Kunstler to use when they would be allowed back in court and could cross-examine.

Henderson, following an agreement with civilian counsel made the previous night, delivered a protest:

> The Manual also requires that civilian counsel be given normal opportunity to attend these proceedings. I would note that this hearing was docketed less than seven days prior to yesterday, and done unilaterally, without consultation with either civilian counsel or military counsel. At great expense, I might add, civilian counsel were able to make it to the hearing yesterday to register their objections to going forward in any manner. Civilian counsel made a heroic effort to make it to the hearing yesterday, given the short docketing time.
>
> We object to proceeding any further in the Article 32 investigation based on yesterday's objections: the

civilian counsel's lack of access. Were they here, they
would have to walk out the door right now anyway.
   I'm here and cleared, but I and Captain Strotman
have not had adequate time to prepare.

Nevertheless, Nourie decided to proceed.

HENDERSON: Mr. Investigating Officer, in order to preserve Sergeant Lonetree's objection to this hearing continuing any
   further, I have been directed by lead counsel in the case not
   to take any further action or any further affirmative part in
   this Article 32 investigation.
NOURIE: You will, along with the assistant counsel, remain present in this hearing room, will you not?
HENDERSON: Yes, sir. Solely because I assume we have to.
NOURIE: I think that is a correct assumption.

Major Short called the government's first witness to the stand:
David Moyer, a scholarly-looking special agent in hornrimmed
glasses. Like most of the intelligence agents throughout the proceedings, he wore what I can only describe as the unofficial spy
uniform: blue blazer and gray slacks.

SHORT: Mr. Moyer, is it correct that you are a special agent for
   the Naval Investigative Service?
MOYER: That is correct.
SHORT: Would you describe how your investigation began in this
   case?
MOYER: Yes, sir. On the morning of the twenty-third of December, I was ordered to attend a briefing at the regional office
   in London, England. At that time, I was told that an individual
   by the name of Sergeant Lonetree apparently had contact
   with Soviet intelligence while assigned as a Marine Security
   Guard in the American Embassy in Moscow, and also in Vienna. Following the briefing, myself and two of my agents,
   Special Agent Hardgrove and Special Agent Sperber, caught

a plane to Vienna, at which time the investigation commenced.

This Article 32 hearing testimony comes from a 419-page transcript filled with many deletions for "national security reasons." Instead of what witnesses then proceeded to say, one reads "REMOVED ON DIRECTION OF THE CIA AS IT CANNOT BE DECLASSIFIED IN ITS ENTIRETY"; "REMOVED BY THE DEPARTMENT OF STATE AS DISCLOSURE WOULD BE DAMAGING TO U.S. NATIONAL SECURITY"; "NOT RELEASED BY DEPARTMENT OF STATE AS CONTENTS COULD NOT BE DECLASSIFIED"; "REMOVED BY NIS ON REVIEW AS IT CONTAINED, IN ITS ENTIRETY, INFORMATION THAT WOULD DAMAGE U.S. NATIONAL SECURITY"; "PAGES 164–193, INCLUSIVE, REMOVED AS RELEASE WOULD REVEAL DETAILS ABOUT COMMUNICATIONS SECURITY SYSTEMS AS WELL AS U.S. ACTIVITIES ABROAD WHICH WOULD DAMAGE U.S. NATIONAL SECURITY. REMOVED BY DEPARTMENT OF STATE"; etc. Or simply nothing, just white-space-minus-testimony, with no explanation.

If an appeal were to become necessary, hardly a farfetched idea even at this early point with the military component of the defense refusing to take part in the proceedings and the civilian component not even present for reasons of security clearance, Clayton's counsel would have a very incomplete record from which to work.

Special Agent Moyer testified primarily about Lonetree's confession in London, sailing along smoothly with no objections from the defense.

Then Prosecutor Short ventured a bit afield:

SHORT: Are you familiar with a defense request for the production of Miss Violetta Sanni, Mr. Aleksiy Yefimov, and Mr. Yuriy Lysov as witnesses for those proceedings?

MOYER: Yes, sir.

SHORT: What is the probable location of these individuals?

MOYER: The first two individuals, to my knowledge, are currently in Moscow. The third is currently in Vienna.

SHORT: What if any difficulties would be encountered by an attempt to produce these individuals?

Moyer's answer is lost, deleted from the record for "national security reasons." Actually, and most interestingly, I was to learn that at the approximate time Short questioned Moyer, Aleksiy Yefimov—Uncle Sasha—was meeting with Shaun Byrnes, a political officer with the State Department assigned to Moscow. Byrnes would admit to being a CIA intern early in his career, while contending that he'd done no work for the Agency in years.

Why was Shaun Byrnes meeting with Uncle Sasha? Why else but to play the role of double agent, the very role Clayton had hoped to be playing.

SHORT: Are you familiar with the defense request to produce the employment record of Violetta Sanni for the period she worked at the U.S. Embassy in Moscow?

MOYER: Yes, sir, I am.

SHORT: What if any attempts have been made to secure that record?

MOYER: Well, the State Department reported Miss Sanni had been fired from her job in December, and a search of their employment records at the embassy in Moscow determined the record had been inadvertently destroyed some time in December.

Inadvertently destroyed? The farce was well underway.

Lonetree's confessions, basically as I've already outlined, were entered into evidence. Henderson and Strotman, as planned with civilian counsel, entered no objection "at this time." With those key words, they refused to cross-examine.

Short called Gunnery Sgt. Darrell J. Enderlin to the stand. Enderlin, dressed in fatigues, looked snappy and clean-cut, as could be said of all the Marines who were to testify. Enderlin had been commander in Vienna of Clayton's MSG detachment.

The witness testified that Clayton had signed a form titled Fraternization with Nationals of a Bloc Country, thereby making his subsequent contacts with the Soviets illegal. The defense had no quarrel with this. We were prepared to admit Lonetree's guilt under the fraternization rules, while pointing out that the vast majority of government employees at the U.S. Embassy in Moscow had such illegal contacts.

Next the prosecution called Eric Scott, an MSG squad leader in Vienna, to show that Clayton *could have* committed the crimes with which he was charged. He had the opportunity, of course. As had every other Marine guard in Moscow.

SHORT: How well did Sergeant Lonetree comply with the recall procedures?

SCOTT: Well, sir, when he would call and check out, I remember a few times when he would say he was going for a walk. I would ask him where, and he would say, "I'm just going for a walk."

SHORT: What was he supposed to tell you?

SCOTT: He is supposed to give a specific location, the destination.

Again Henderson and Strotman refused to cross-examine. Investigating Officer Nourie, pressing ahead, had to wonder about the hearing's value in view of the absence of civilian defense counsel, and the refusal to cross-examine by Lonetree's military counsel.

Stuhff, upon learning what had transpired, expressed confidence that Enderlin and Scott's testimony—consisting mostly of suggestions that Lonetree had had opportunity, plus, in Enderlin's case, that Clayton should have reported his contacts—could be nullified, even turned to the defense's advantage. On the other hand, the confessions had been admitted into evidence.

With the defense effectively muffled, Stuhff and Kunstler were of a mind that even a whit of fairness demanded that Clayton's confessions, and thus the entire case, be thrown out.

Nourie, perhaps thinking the same thing, adjourned the Article 32 hearing until the next day. Maybe those security clearances would have come through by then.

February 6, 1987
1315 HOURS

NOURIE: I believe we left much as we started yesterday, save of course the production of the evidence as far as the limited access to be granted, if any, to Mr. Kunstler and Mr. Stuhff. Enlighten us on that, Major Short.

SHORT: First, on the issue of access. The national agency checks on all three civilian parties has been completed. The results of those national agency checks are now being reviewed by the Commander, Naval Security Investigative Command. Upon his determination of whether General Petersen is authorized to grant or deny access, and upon General Petersen's action, the Investigating Officer will be advised immediately, as well as the defense, but I do not have that information as yet.

NOURIE: Does the government desire to rest its case at this point?

SHORT: No, sir.

NOURIE: Major Henderson, do you have anything to say?

HENDERSON: No, sir. As far as the defense position, we're still waiting for an answer. I renew all objections to the proceedings of yesterday and Wednesday. I also have received and would like to introduce into evidence what has previously been marked as Investigative Exhibit 27, which is a Western Union mailgram from the lead counsel, Mr. Stuhff. I would like to introduce it into the record to note that the objections made by myself to the proceedings yesterday were concurred in by the civilian counsel in this case.

A comedy? A tragedy? We could only wonder how an objective observer—had any been allowed in that hearing room—would have viewed the proceedings. As anything other than a travesty? Facts such as the names of Clayton's parents and the date of his enlistment in the Marines had been declared secret, knowledge of them labeled a risk to "national security." The defense couldn't defend. Even its client's confessions were classified top secret.

But matters would get worse, much worse, as a powerful government, afraid to admit it had created a monstrous sham, plunged forward.

Major Nourie, a small, probably unknowing cog in the huge government apparatus surrounding and zeroing in on Lonetree, called a recess for the weekend.

9

THE PRESS LEAKS BEGIN

February 9, 1987
1428 H O U R S

NOURIE: I believe when we left this matter, we were still waiting for information as to granting limited access and declassification of certain documents.

SHORT: Mr. Investigating Officer, the status of both of those issues is that I am unable to pin down a time when action on either concern will be completed. I would simply state that immediately upon receipt of the decisions on either one of these, I will make available to the defense anything that I receive within the appropriate level of classification.

HENDERSON: Mr. Investigating Officer, the defense's position is that matters raised by defense counsel on Wednesday, the first session of the case, have still not been addressed by the government to allow the defense to proceed. We are still in no better position than we were on Wednesday to go ahead in this case because of the lack of information, lack of answer to the questions, and lack of provided discovery to the accused.

If only the press could have been there. But more to the point of the whole frustrating situation, I had to wonder what was going on behind the scenes. Our mighty government, able to respond instantly to international crises anywhere around the globe, was bogged down in bureaucracy over the declassification of a few documents.

Legally, at least, the government had reason to hurry: that ninety-day deadline. Perhaps someone on high had said, "Damned if I'll break my back for Bill Kunstler," but if so he was trading small satisfaction for the likelihood of a big defeat down the line. Or maybe, hidden in the recesses of power, there was someone who really did believe that vital secrets were at stake. Who could say, who could know what was really going on?

Clayton himself so far had been passive, quiet, eager to please. A nice young man. The perfect Marine. He followed suggestions and didn't say much. Occasionally he passed notes to his military counsel. Invariably he agreed with defense strategy, harboring his secret hopes, yet resigned to whatever was to be.

Clayton's vulnerability shone for the world to see, if the world had been allowed to see. It would have been hard to imagine anyone in that hearing room mistaking this obviously guileless young man as a master spy.

February 12, 1987
1428 H O U R S

Still the clearances hadn't come through.

And how the press blackout was breached.

While still bent on denying information to the hobbled defense, government officials had provided plenty to at least one member of the press, including full disclosure of Clayton's "classified" background. The day after the last session of the hearing, February 10, the following article by Bill McAllister had appeared in the *Washington Post:*

At 25, Sgt. Clayton John Lonetree appeared to be the stuff of which Marine Corps recruiting ads are made: an average high school student, a second-string football player who had been molded by the Corps' tough discipline into an exceptional serviceman.

"Lonetree stands tall at the summit," proclaimed the *St. Paul Pioneer Press* when he was dispatched from the U.S. Embassy in Moscow to serve in the honor guard at the 1985 summit between President Reagan and Soviet leader Mikhail Gorbachev.

In late December, however, the Marine, son of a well-known Indian leader in Minnesota, called his superiors aside and another aspect of his life as an Embassy Guard in Moscow, and later Vienna, began to emerge. Two weeks ago Marine Corps officials charged Lonetree with espionage, making him the first Marine Guard to be accused of spying in the 38 years that Marines have been protecting U.S. embassies.

While Marine Corps officials will not describe what Lonetree has said, interview with Defense and State Department sources indicate that he apparently volunteered that, while in Moscow, he became sexually involved with a Soviet woman whose name in English is Violetta Sanni and who worked in the embassy as a translator.

On Jan. 27, a Marine Corps major walked into the brig and presented Lonetree with a five-page, single-spaced typewritten form, Defense Department Form 458. It accused Lonetree of espionage, a crime punishable by death, and other offenses for dealing with Sanni and two other Soviet agents, called "Uncle Sasha" and "George."

Defense and State Department officials have said the disclosures in the Lonetree case caused "serious damage" to national security, although last week one State Department source said the formal charges may indicate that the damage may not have been "as drastic" as initial accounts suggested. Some reports had implied that Lonetree helped Soviet agents enter the Moscow embassy and plant listening devices, and that he "told the Soviets of the building's espionage safe-guards."

Defense and State Department sources: while we were being kept in the dark, these worthies were talking to the *Washington Post*. On the point of future disclosures, however, the article was pessimistic:

> The story of how Lonetree, son of a Winnebago father and a Navajo mother, fell may never be made public. A Marine Corps spokesman said that the closed pretrial hearing could indicate that if Lonetree goes on trial, it too will be closed.

Finally, the article got into the area of reactions from Lonetree's family, particularly his brother Craig:

> . . . Lonetree picked Vienna as his second post, his brother said, because he wanted to learn more about Europe. In his only public interview at Quantico, Lonetree told his cousin, a reporter on the Traverse City, Mich., *Record-Eagle*, that his reasons for seeking guard duty were simple: "I wanted to see the world."
> What will happen now? Craig Lonetree paused and said he understands that his brother faces a possible death sentence.
> But, he continued, the military had not executed anyone in peacetime for spying. "They'll probably give him a life sentence. You have to look at it positively."

If hope of a life sentence was an example of positive thinking, the government had already succeeded in crucifying Clayton Lonetree, and with judicial proceedings barely underway. In any case, unwilling to proceed with actual testimony, the February 12 session of the Article 32 hearing—Stuhff, Kunstler, and myself still absent—devoted itself to talk about trips to Vienna and Moscow by a junket combining prosecution and defense. If the mountain wouldn't come to Mohammed . . .

March 5, 1987
1408 H O U R S

A superstar of sorts, described to me as a "heavy hitter" of military jurisprudence, joined the prosecution as lead government counsel. Marine Maj. David Beck was viewed in military circles in the exalted way civilians might look on F. Lee Bailey, Racehorse Haynes, or, yes, William Kunstler.

In his late thirties, short, with blond hair and a smooth southern accent, Beck used a polite, soft-spoken demeanor to hide a prosecutorial instinct for the jugular. Military lawyers didn't come any better than Beck. Well-read, he could quote the Latin poet Juvenal as readily as he might a point of legal precedent, and his taking over as head prosecutor was further demonstration, the clearest yet, of the government's determination to convict Lonetree.

Among the many notches on David Beck's gun: he was the only navy prosecutor ever to obtain a death sentence in a court-martial.

We had no doubt that Beck was looking for a second in his prosecution of Clayton Lonetree.

Major Beck's entrance into the case overshadowed even the granting of clearances to Kunstler and Stuhff—a positive development clouded by the government's refusal to give the same to me.

Henderson, with the civilian defense team still absent this day, protested: "There has been no decision on Mr. Headley's access. Based upon the government's failure to provide access to our investigator, and based on the long period of time it took them to provide access to civilian counsel, the defense is compelled by the government's lack of diligence in this case to request a continuance of the Article 32 hearing."

How important was I? Was General Petersen, or someone above him, afraid of what I might learn with my own security clearance? I stood as just one man, but still the only man registered as an investigator for Clayton. On the other side, the government enjoyed the services of scores of fully-cleared investigators.

No arrangements had been made for the Article 32 participants to journey to Moscow or Vienna, and the March 5 session was largely devoted to bickering over where the blame belonged. The State Department contended it couldn't secure the necessary visas from Moscow. Purportedly the Soviets were stonewalling, retaliating for the arrest of one of their own after they had taken Nicholas Daniloff into custody; virtually all travel between the two countries had slowed to a trickle.

The ninety-day clock continued to run as Nourie again recessed the hearing. For the next session, the defense expected a wild and surprising maneuver from Beck, the dynamic new prosecutor, and sure enough it came.

10

RESETTING THE CLOCK

March 26, 1987
1335 H O U R S

Beck's bombshell dropped right at the start of the day's proceedings.

"I have been presented this morning," Nourie said, "with additional charges in this case, and Additional Charge One alleges conspiracy to commit espionage, two specifications; Additional Charge Two indicating espionage violation of Article 106a, one specification; and the Additional Charge Three, violation of article 134, the first specification being an assimilation of certain U.S. Code provisions pertaining to espionage, and the second specification being that of unlawful entry."

Beck had won the government a fresh ninety days by piling additional charges on Lonetree at the last minute!

Clayton had been in solitary confinement since New Year's Day—itself a violation of his constitutional rights according to a Supreme Court ruling which established that more than thirty days in solitary constituted cruel and unusual punishment—and now the government was reloading to come after him with new ammunition. And most curious of all, the new charges had been officially filed two days ago, on March 24, exactly ninety days since Clayton's formal arrest and incarceration.

Beck's bombshell was nothing less than revelation of an alleged full-scale spy ring as part of a so-called Moscow spy scandal, with Clayton supposedly at the center along with another more recently arrested Marine who had served at the embassy concurrently, Cpl. Arnold Bracy.

Corporal Bracy, son of a black fundamentalist minister, was arrested on March 20, 1987, at the Marine base at Twenty-nine Palms, California, after three days of grueling, relentless NIS interrogation. The NIS went after Bracy because it had decided that Clayton alone couldn't have done everything with which he was charged (mainly what he had "confessed" to Agent Brannon after being urged to lie). In addition to charges of fraternization, Bracy was accused, together with Lonetree and others implicated in Bracy's reported confession (themselves then brutally interrogated, though not eventually arrested or publicly charged), of allowing KGB agents free access to roam the embassy after dark, among other less publicized offenses.

What actually happened: as Bracy wore down under his interrogation, NIS agents asked him to speculate on various scenarios, then took down his responses as fact and badgered him into signing the resulting "confession" without reading it.

"They told me," Bracy would eventually state, " 'If you don't sign this, your life will be over as an American citizen. At age twenty-one your life will be over. Just sign here.' " Bracy added: "So like a dummy I signed."

Not only did Bracy's arrest serve to reset Clayton's ninety-day clock, it also signaled an all-out attempt by the government to try Clayton (and Bracy) in the press with a flood of the very kind of leaks officials had statedly feared from the defense in the denials of our security clearances. The *Washington Post* was the main clarion of these new "revelations," which had been kept from the Lonetree defense until the March 26 proceedings, when Beck dutifully passed them on to Mike Stuhff (Kunstler had urgent business elsewhere, and I hadn't yet been cleared). That same day, the *Post* began a virtually daily series of articles on the case.

March 26, 1987
THE WASHINGTON POST

The arrest of a second Marine suspected of espionage while working as a U.S. Embassy Guard in Moscow has triggered a wide-ranging security probe at the embassy, the State Department said yesterday.

"We are treating this as a very serious breach of our security," spokesman Charles E. Redman said, referring to the arrest of Cpl. Arnold Bracy, 21, of Queens, NY.

"A full-scale counterintelligence investigation is being conducted in coordination with other appropriate federal agencies. We're looking at every aspect of security in the embassy in Moscow," Redman said.

March 27, 1987
THE WASHINGTON POST

The Reagan administration has begun a high-level and hardball reevaluation of security procedures at the U.S. Embassy in Moscow that could lead to substantial changes in methods used to protect all American embassies located in East bloc countries, State Department sources said yesterday.

U.S. investigators are trying to determine whether the two Marine Guards, Cpl. Arnold Bracy and Sgt. Clayton J. Lonetree, acting separately or together, allowed Soviet intelligence agents access to the Embassy Chancery Building at night.

As a result of the Guards' arrests, U.S. officials are considering the possibility that the two Marines, rather than CIA defector Edward L. Howard, provided the Soviets with some of the information about U.S. intelligence operations in Moscow that enabled the Soviets to seriously impair U.S. information-gathering there.

March 28, 1987
THE WASHINGTON POST

The two Marine Corps guards accused of espionage gave Soviet agents access to the U.S. Embassy's most sensitive areas and cryptographic equipment in Moscow, military prosecutors said yesterday.

The disclosures, contained in five additional charges filed against one of the two servicemen, suggest that the United States may have suffered one of its worse security breaches in recent years.

One Capitol Hill source said the action would once again devastate U.S. intelligence operations in Moscow, which were said to have been crippled after the defection of a former Central Intelligence Agency agent in 1985.

The two Marine Guards, who allegedly were sexually involved with two Soviet women who worked at the U.S. Embassy, allegedly committed the espionage between January and March of 1986, according to military prosecutors.

"You got to start from ground zero, whole new people and a whole new system all over again," the Capitol Hill source said.

March 29, 1987
THE WASHINGTON POST

Defense Secretary Caspar W. Weinberger said yesterday that the United States suffered "a very great loss" from Soviet agents rooting through secret areas of the U.S. Embassy in Moscow under an arrangement allegedly permitted by two Marine Corps Guards.

"We're very, very distressed," Weinberger said in an interview on the Cable News Network, referring to what military prosecutors have described as a secrets-for-sex operation at the embassy.

So Defense and State Department sources had been joined by the Marine Corps, military prosecutors, and Capitol Hill mouthpieces, with Major Nourie all the while continuing to remind the defense of the secrecy of the Article 32 hearing.

Even President Ronald Reagan was hauled into the act, something I discovered myself after learning the codename "Cabin Boy" for the Marine Guard investigation. Given that lead, I uncovered the following NIS memo:

PRESIDENT REAGAN HAS BEEN BRIEFED ON THE CASE. EXPRESSED CONCERN AND REQUESTED FREQUENT UP-DATES. AS SUCH, THIS INVESTIGATION TAKES PRIORITY OVER ANY MATTER NOW BEING HANDLED BY NIS AND MUST BE RESPONDED TO ACCORDINGLY.

The *Washington Post,* quickly joined by hundreds of major newspapers worldwide and echoed by the drumbeat of radio and television reports of this "major spy scandal," finally convinced Clayton to abandon his naive hope for a quiet burial or fading away of the case—but not his belief that somehow he might yet become a double agent.

While Mike Stuhff was still digesting the new charges against Lonetree on March 26, Prosecutor Beck, given a new ninety days with which to work, reopened the government case by calling Kenneth C. Kidwell, Department of State.

Prompted by Beck, Kidwell testified at length about devices that encipher and decipher, cryptographic materials, super-advanced equipment, data systems and computers—all available in the U.S. Embassy in Moscow, all within reach of Marine guards.

In other words, again, Lonetree had opportunity.

Stuhff began his first cross-examination of a government witness.

STUHFF: Did any key cryptographic software information come up missing?
KIDWELL: No, sir.

STUHFF: Are there any indications it was compromised?

KIDWELL: No, sir.

STUHFF: Was there any indication the keying material was compromised?

KIDWELL: I have no knowledge of a compromise.

STUHFF: And, there is no indication that anything was ever compromised?

KIDWELL: I am aware of no instance where material has been compromised.

STUHFF: Are you in a position to know if it had been compromised?

KIDWELL: I believe I am.

STUHFF: What about the material you indicated you are responsible for—the hardware, the machines—did any of that material come up missing?

KIDWELL: No, sir. No missing material of any variety.

So much for the State Department's Kenneth Kidwell.

Next came the defense's turn at David Moyer, the scholarly-looking NIS agent wearing his blue blazer and gray slacks. Moyer's previously unchallenged testimony had led to the acceptance of Clayton's confessions into evidence, so Stuhff's cross-examination of Moyer carried great importance.

STUHFF: When did you first become acquainted with Sergeant Clayton Lonetree?

MOYER: That would have been the evening of 24 December 1986. In a coffee shop at the Intercontinental Hotel in Vienna, Austria.

STUHFF: Who was present?

MOYER: Myself, Sergeant Lonetree, Special Agent Hardgrove, and Special Agent Sperber from my London office.

STUHFF: What time did this meeting take place?

MOYER: Approximately six o'clock in the evening.

STUHFF: When you were introduced to Sergeant Lonetree, what did you say to him?

MOYER: I said, "Good evening, Sergeant. Nice to meet you." We sat down and I asked him if he wanted a glass of orange juice or a cup of coffee. He asked for a glass of orange juice. I had a cup of coffee myself. We engaged in a very limited social conversation, and Sergeant Lonetree accompanied me and the two agents back to a different hotel.

STUHFF: The purpose of the limited social conversation was to set Sergeant Lonetree at ease, correct?

MOYER: Just to arrange a social—that is a difficult question.

STUHFF: To establish a rapport?

MOYER: Yes, that is correct. Basically so he would know us, and we would know him.

STUHFF: So you would be able to sit down and talk together in a friendly manner.

MOYER: I would say basically so he would know that we represented the United States Government.

STUHFF: You had some social banter or conversation?

MOYER: Yes.

STUHFF: Do you recall the subject of that social conversation?

MOYER: Life in Vienna, the weather, Christmas.

STUHFF: Did you discuss with Sergeant Lonetree anything relating to his contact with Russian nationals in that particular conversation?

MOYER: Not at that time, no.

STUHFF: Did you advise Sergeant Lonetree that he had a right not to incriminate himself?

MOYER: Not at that time.

STUHFF: If Sergeant Lonetree had stood up in that coffee shop and walked out, would you have allowed him to do that?

MOYER: We would have gone with him.

STUHFF: So he would remain subject to your control and custody?

MOYER: That is correct.

STUHFF: So, after you had this social banter and conversation and some refreshments, I assume at some point you stood up?

MOYER: We went outside the hotel and caught a taxi back to the Hotel Strudelhof, also located in Vienna.

STUHFF: Would you describe where everybody sat in this taxi?

MOYER: I believe I sat in the front with the driver, and Special Agent Hardgrove, Special Agent Sperber, and Sergeant Lonetree sat in the rear.

STUHFF: And Sergeant Lonetree sat in the center of the rear seat, is that correct?

MOYER: I believe so.

STUHFF: You do recall that is correct because the other special agents by prearrangement sat on either side of him?

MOYER: It is normal procedure.

STUHFF: The plan was that he would be in the center of the back seat?

MOYER: Yes.

STUHFF: And again, that is so he would not—if something should occur—open the door and run off. Is that the reason for the procedure?

MOYER: I would say yes.

Stuhff's questioning made clear that they had, in effect, arrested Clayton, only he didn't know it. And he had a legal right to know. The point went right to the heart of the confessions, which were the *only* evidence against Clayton, and therefore the reason this Article 32 was so important. Throw the confessions out and the case goes with it.

STUHFF: What transpired in that room?

MOYER: I advised Sergeant Lonetree at that time I was a special agent with the Naval Investigative Service, and I advised him he was suspected of the offenses. In fact there was a pre-printed military suspect's acknowledgment and waiver of rights form which I then took out, and advised the Sergeant what he was suspected of.

But Clayton didn't understand! He was hoping to become a double agent. In fact, Clayton didn't realize he'd been arrested until he reached the Quantico brig on New Year's Eve. A confused kid, yes. A traitor, no.

STUHFF: How was Sergeant Lonetree dressed at this time?

MOYER: In casual clothes.

STUHFF: Who else was present in the room with you? Special Agent Sperber?

MOYER: That is correct.

STUHFF: How was Special Agent Sperber dressed?

MOYER: In casual clothes, the best I can recall. I believe a sweater with a shirt and a pair of slacks.

STUHFF: Did you have in your possession any restraining devices?

MOYER: Yes, we did.

STUHFF: Handcuffs?

MOYER: That is correct.

STUHFF: And how were you carrying your handcuffs?

MOYER: They were in Mr. Sperber's briefcase.

Hidden from Clayton, though ready to be brought out should Clayton wake up to the fact that he was under arrest. Until then, however, they would let him go on, believing he was talking to friends.

STUHFF: Sergeant Lonetree volunteered to go back to the Soviet Union under control of the United States as a double agent. Correct?

MOYER: He mentioned that during the interview, yes.

STUHFF: Was he warned there would be substantial dangers if he did that?

MOYER: He was advised that a situation like that in an Iron Bloc country or a Soviet Bloc country, where we would have no control to help him, would be very dangerous.

If they wanted to be up front and honest, why not just say, "Look, Lonetree, we know you're a traitor. Forget this double-agent bullshit."

STUHFF: And despite that danger to himself, communicated to him by agents of our government, he still volunteered to undertake that particular duty?

MOYER: He said he would be willing to do it. Specifically, I recall, he wanted to find Howard for us.

STUHFF: You asked Sergeant Lonetree on Christmas Eve if he would mind staying with you and Special Agent Sperber in a room that had been arranged for the purpose of interrogating him. Correct?

MOYER: That is correct.

STUHFF: The following morning you went to London?

MOYER: That is correct.

STUHFF: Did Sergeant Lonetree have a set of clothes or any baggage that he happened to be carrying with him at the time?

MOYER: Yes, he did.

STUHFF: Where did they come from?

MOYER: The Marine House.

STUHFF: How did they get to him?

MOYER: One of the Marines brought his clothes over to us.

STUHFF: So there had to be a special arrangement made to have his clothes brought over to you?

MOYER: Oh, yes.

Certainly they wouldn't have allowed Lonetree, clearly unaware that he was under arrest, to fetch his clothes. He might have told a friendly Marine what was happening and gotten the good advice to stop talking and seek legal help.

STUHFF: If Sergeant Lonetree had decided to leave your company at this time, was he free to do it?

MOYER: If Sergeant Lonetree had at any point invoked his rights to a lawyer or his right to remain silent, he would have been apprehended.

STUHFF: That is a different question than what I asked. If he had decided to leave your presence, would he have been free to leave?

MOYER: No.

STUHFF: So it was fair to say he was not free to leave?

MOYER: That is correct.

Again, he was under arrest and didn't know it.

STUHFF: How long was Sergeant Lonetree kept at the suite at the Heathrow Holiday Inn?

MOYER: From Christmas Day until he was flown out of England. Which I believe was the 30th. No, actually he left, I believe, the 29th. But he was turned over to the Marine barracks in London. That would be four days.

STUHFF: During those several days that he was maintained near the London airport at the Holiday Inn, he was again interrogated several times. Is that correct?

MOYER: That is correct.

STUHFF: Did you observe Special Agent Brannon interrogating Sergeant Lonetree?

MOYER: I participated with Special Agent Brannon in the interview of the sergeant.

STUHFF: Did you or Special Agent Brannon make a suggestion to Sergeant Lonetree that he just tell a lie about his involvement?

MOYER: Yes.

STUHFF: And why did you suggest he tell a lie?

MOYER: Special Agent Brannon, during the course of the second interrogation following Sergeant Lonetree's second statement, said words to the effect, "Clayton, talk to us. Say something. Say something. Hell, just say something, even tell us a lie." At that point Clayton got choked up and said, "What do you want to hear?" We said, "Clayton, just tell us the damn truth, but say something. Now, did you in fact take documents from any of these embassies?" At that point Clayton said, yes, he did.

STUHFF: Why did Special Agent Brannon say, "Just tell us a lie"?

MOYER: I would say to get him talking again. He was sitting very quiet. He wouldn't respond. He looked very remorseful.

STUHFF: That is an assumption you made because he sat there quietly?

MOYER: No. His head was down. He had tears coming down. He looked like a person who wanted to say something, but couldn't get himself to come out with the verbiage. And in an attempt to get Clayton talking or saying anything, that comment was made by Special Agent Brannon.

STUHFF: Have you had any training in psychology, Agent Moyer?

MOYER: I took courses in college.

STUHFF: You are not a psychologist, however?

MOYER: That is correct.

STUHFF: And you and Agent Brannon attempted to re-establish some sort of communication with him?

MOYER: That is correct.

STUHFF: Apparently Agent Brannon attempted to re-establish communication by asking him to tell a lie.

MOYER: That statement was made. Yes, sir.

STUHFF: What was Sergeant Lonetree's appearance and demeanor during this particular interrogation, after the comment by Agent Brannon that he should tell a lie?

MOYER: It became very intense. Sergeant Lonetree, at that point, began to cry, and he appeared to be starting to hyperventilate, taking deep breaths, rapidly. At that point we told him to collect himself. He went into the bathroom and put some water on his face. We just sat down, maybe two or three minutes, until he appeared to be in complete control of himself again, and then we commenced the conversation.

STUHFF: That wasn't the first time he cried or that you saw him cry, was it?

MOYER: That was the strongest he had cried. There had been other times in my contact with Sergeant Lonetree where tears came to his eyes, but this particular occasion he was actually bawling. Heavy tears were rolling down his face. He had difficulty breathing . . . not in breathing, but he was taking deep breaths, and choking sobs were coming from his throat.

STUHFF: One of the methodologies you used to try to elicit the truth from Sergeant Lonetree, for your purposes, was to continue this interrogation over a period of several days. Is that correct?

MOYER: As long as he was willing to talk to us, yes.

STUHFF: And that's why you kept it up through the 25th, 26th, 27th, up to the 29th?

MOYER: That is correct. Up until that time he invoked his rights, at which time all questioning stopped; and if he hadn't invoked at that point, we would have continued.

STUHFF: You would have kept going for days and weeks after that?

MOYER: Well, as long as he was willing to talk to us.

Subject to a lengthy, relentless interrogation by NIS agents, unaware of being under arrest, Clayton made statements to people he trusted—representatives of his own government. His emotional breakdown under that interrogation, which Moyer and the prosecution might interpret as evidence of guilt, was no more excessive than the reactions of other Moscow MSGs similarly interrogated who were eventually determined innocent of any charges. And a number of the statements Clayton made to the NIS, after being urged to lie, the prosecution itself knew couldn't be true.

Eventually, reporter Pete Earley, writing in the *Washington Post Magazine* on Feb. 7, 1988, pointed out "that nearly *everything*" in Clayton's just-tell-us-a-lie confession "was untrue, and, in many cases, that it would have been physically *impossible* for him to have done what he confessed." But "the NIS had used the third confession [which included Clayton's only "admission" of having stolen top-secret documents] to spark the sex-for-secrets scandal, which proved impossible to squelch."

Why was it impossible to squelch? The truth would have squelched it. But the truth would have required that the government tell the truth, that it admit to errors. And clearly no one on the government side was going to volunteer such an admission.

"The NIS made another supposition," Earley wrote. "Lonetree must have had a partner. He didn't seem bright enough to have acted alone. The suspect they chose was Marine Cpl. Arnold Bracy, who served in Moscow with Lonetree and had gotten into trouble for unauthorized contact with Soviets."

"Unauthorized": in other words, Bracy had had an affair with a Soviet woman.

As did Lonetree.

You had to wonder . . . here were these Marine guards, young, virile, in excellent physical shape. They had to be single—a job requirement—and to take an oath *not to marry for three years.* This effectively killed any hope for a lasting relationship with a girlfriend back home. Imagine: "Well, honey, I'm headed for Moscow and God knows where else, but you just wait three years for me."

Then the Marine guards were told not to fraternize with any Soviet national. How was a Marine to know? ("Check for bad breath and poor quality shoes," the indoctrinating sergeant had said.) Soviet women, in bars frequented by Marine guards, could and did say, "Soviet? I'm from Finland." Or Sweden. Or wherever. Could anyone expect a healthy young man not yet ready for celibacy to run a nationality check?

Women were everywhere in Moscow, especially around the U.S. Embassy, and some undoubtedly worked for the Soviet government and seduced U.S. Marines. In a realistic world, where should the blame have been placed?

After the testimony of Agent Moyer, Investigating Officer Nourie recessed the proceedings to give civilian defense counsel a chance to interview future witnesses. What we found would shock the most jaded observer of diplomatic personnel on duty abroad.

11

FUNDS RAISED, MOTIONS DENIED

Money remained a continuing problem for the defense, despite three fundraising rallies for Clayton held between February and July.

The first took place in St. Paul, Minnesota on February 27 and drew about a hundred people, mainly Native Americans. Set up by Spencer Lonetree and his sister Kathy, both of whom worked tirelessly for Clayton, it was held in the American Indian Center, an old and dilapidated building—inevitably so, for these were poor people—where the audience had to sit on creaking, ancient folding chairs. Yet it was filled with rapt faces as William Kunstler spoke, and one couldn't fail to be moved by these people coming together for one of their own.

Kunstler had lived a year in the Twin Cities during the Wounded Knee trials, and his presence had guaranteed press coverage. "Clayton's alliance with the woman," the *Minneapolis Star and Tribune* quoted from his speech the next day, "may have been an act of misjudgment on his part, but to say he gave any secrets away, as Defense Secretary Caspar Weinberger says, is just hogwash."

Always an effective speaker, Kunstler had stiff competition this night. Clayton's grandfather Sam, a revered Winnebago holy man—tall, distinguished-looking, articulate, his hair worn in long braids—brought tears to the eyes of most in the crowd. Honor and honesty creased into his lined face, Sam Lonetree told about Clayton asking his permission to join the Marine Corps, and recounted the Lonetrees' tradition of brave service to their country: besides Congressional Medal of Honor winner Mitchell Red Cloud, other illustrious military heroes in Clayton's family included John Hill (Civil War) and Hugh Lonetree (World War I).

"Clayton wanted to follow in the tradition of Mitchell Red Cloud," Sam Lonetree told the assemblage.

Spencer Lonetree also moved the audience by describing Clayton's love of children. At the embassy in Moscow, Spencer related, other Marine guards chased small children away, but Clayton always kept candy bars on hand to pass out to them.

Spencer told about buying his son a rifle and taking him deer hunting. "But Clayton didn't want to kill those beautiful animals," Spencer said. "That's the kind of person my son is."

The rally raised sixty dollars—a sacrifice for the Indians, but one that lifted all our spirits.

The second fundraiser came on March 27, the day after Stuhff's cross-examination of NIS agent Moyer, in Denver, Colorado. Kathy Lonetree had asked Mike Stuhff and me to come and plead for help at a major powwow of Midwest and Western tribes at the Denver Coliseum. Six thousand Native Americans would be attending.

The powwow, similar to the white man's county fair, featured dance competitions, exhibitions, selling and trading Indian objects, and reunion of old friends.

I felt terrible about going there to ask for money: *a white guy, for God's sake,* I thought, *begging poor people to give him cash.*

Stuhff felt the same way. "I'm not good at this," he said, "and my heart's not in it."

Sam Lonetree and his wife Annie came to Denver to join us at the powwow, as did Clayton's father, Spencer.

A blanket dance, traditional at Native American weddings—where the Indians throw money on a blanket for the newlyweds—

became the vehicle for our fundraising, and the ceremony served to lighten our feelings about our purpose there.

We managed to raise all of $212, but that was a considerable amount, even with so many Indians present. Few people in this country realize how destitute most Native Americans are.

Bill Kunstler brought a star to the third and final fundraiser, arranged by Spencer Lonetree and held July 17 at the Holiday Inn State Capitol in St. Paul.

Kunstler ran into Arlo Guthrie on the plane from New York to St. Paul. Guthrie was to perform at the Twin Cities' Riverfest, and Bill told the singer about his trip's purpose. Guthrie, famously generous with his time for just causes, volunteered to perform.

By this time, Stuhff and I were scraping near bottom in the personal finance department. I was looking to find a buyer for my car so I could continue on the case, and Stuhff, the night before flying to St. Paul, found himself in a situation guaranteed to test his humiliation quotient. His family wanted to see the movie *Roxanne,* and he didn't have the twenty dollars to take them. He had to borrow the money from his fourteen-year-old daughter Mischa's baby-sitting savings to take her, his wife Sandy, and son Joe, age nine, to the film. It preyed on his mind all the way to St. Paul—a lawyer, thirty-nine years old, without twenty dollars—and he began to wonder whether Sandy, always openly supportive, even during all the hard years working on the reservation, really approved of his going on. He had eight dollars on him, flying to St. Paul, and knew he'd have to find a motel and eating places that wouldn't check his charged-to-the-limit credit cards. And after St. Paul lay still several other months in D.C. and Quantico.

My own heart sank in St. Paul when I saw once again a crowd of predominantly Native Americans at the Holiday Inn State Capitol. Spencer and Kathy Lonetree had done a great job of drumming up attendance, but again the crowd lacked the faces of rich white liberals.

The meeting raised twelve hundred dollars, a lot more than the first two, thanks largely to Arlo Guthrie's stirring and appropriate rendition of "This Land is Your Land," but it still left me with a bad feeling about myself. It just wasn't right to ask people with so very little to contribute to my livelihood.

The twelve hundred dollars helped, but matters really improved at the airport the next day while we were waiting for the flight to Washington, D.C. Craig Lonetree, Clayton's brother, showed up to present us with a most welcome surprise: a $3,500 check from the Lonetree Defense Fund, primarily acquired through Spencer's Herculean money-raising efforts over the past several months.

April 15, 1987
0938 H O U R S

My clearance had finally come through! So this day I found myself sitting at the defense table in the tightly guarded basement room, next to Clayton.

The hearing today had begun with a buzz of excitement after the discovery that a Washington, D.C., reporter had sneaked in to view the proceedings. Coincidentally, one of two defense motions pending this morning related to the press.

Kunstler argued the first motion with his usual commanding presence: let the press see what was going on. After citing the Constitution and a host of legal precedent, Kunstler showed how denying the media access to the proceeding had only led to false reporting:

> We've had a variety of extensive publicity about Sergeant Lonetree. I've brought a great deal of it from my home city of New York. It has been front-page, and I'm just holding up some of it to the court: "Pentagon Claims Marines Led Reds on Spy Tour" with a picture of Sergeant Lonetree and Corporal Bracy in our *Daily News*, the largest circulation paper in New York. Another headline states, "They Let Spies In, Says U.S.," also "Two Marines Charged in Moonlight Tours." Now, that didn't come from us, the defense. It came from what they call "unidentified Pentagon sources."
>
> As against that, we've maintained silence. The de-

fendant is sealed off, the Commandant of this post has refused to let "60 Minutes" come to interview him, claiming that brig security and national security militate that closure. I know that reporters have not even been permitted on the base, except for that one enterprising gentleman who got through. But they're crowded up at the entrance to the base. Television and print media and radio people are trying to get in.

Keeping this secret only gives a bad impression to the general public. There's really no reason for most of the testimony, and I might add if there is any reason, the Department of Defense, or the Secretary of Defense and others, including members of the Marine Corps, have just dissipated it, by giving out material to the press.

There are people dealing cards in this game, including the Secretary of Defense, and I'm sure this news was filtered out through these people. This is in the *Daily News*, March 27, and it says, "They Wiped Us Out." Now that comes from somebody, and it says, "Pentagon Claims."

I ask most seriously that you go forward today and open this court to the press. If there is a serious question of anything relating to national security that has not already been released by the government, then we can litigate that here today.

Kunstler then took up the second defense motion:

The rule is essentially that an accused must be brought to trial within ninety days from arrest, excluding the day of arrest, or the charges should be dismissed. And I referred you to one case, *United States* v. *Henderson,* where they dismissed a murder charge for failure to bring to trial within the ninety days.

There's no doubt on the initial charges that the ninety days have run. Therefore, putting those by themselves, and not taking into consideration any new charges for the moment, the ninety days have run and the charges should be dismissed.

Kunstler talked about the new charges, all filed on March 24, the ninetieth day after Clayton's arrest. These new charges, all based on statements since recanted by Corporal Bracy, had no merit. Beck must have known that in a fair and open hearing, he would have been likely to lose his case right now. He rose to argue in rebuttal:

> Mr. Investigating Officer, the government's position is that this hearing is not the forum to litigate either motion.
>
> There are numerous military cases establishing the right for closed proceedings. The case cited by Mr. Kunstler, for the main part, the Supreme Court case he referred to, related to a trial.
>
> We are not yet at the trial stage. The most analogous thing to an Article 32 investigation in the civilian world is a Grand Jury hearing. There is no right of the press to attend a Grand Jury hearing. Most of the indictments by the Grand Jury are returned sealed.
>
> As far as Sergeant Lonetree's release from pretrial confinement, I would just say that Rule 707 leaves the determination in this case for the military judge at trial.
>
> Obviously there is going to be some differences between the defense and the government as to who is responsible for getting to this one hundred and twelve day period, and this is not at all the proper forum to litigate anything about pretrial confinement.

Kunstler asked to respond briefly:

> The case in question doesn't pertain to a trial at all. It's a pretrial proceeding. It pertains to a suppression hearing long in advance of trial. And we're not talking about Grand Jury proceedings, which are not adversary proceedings, and which are secret by statute in almost

every state and essentially even by the Constitution of the United States on the federal level. This isn't a Grand Jury proceeding. This is an adversarial proceeding.

I heard the President of the United States discuss this case. I heard the Secretary of State, Secretary Weinberger, and hordes of people going down the rung of command and hierarchy. And the defense is left unable to respond.

We can't say "unidentified sources" to the newspaper. But the Pentagon does, and gets away with it.

We're just asking for an open court. Let the press hear it. If there is something that should be classified, clear the courtroom and we can litigate whether it merits that kind of treatment.

The press is the voice of the community, and the community should hear what's going on. There is enormous public interest.

This is not an AWOL or a desertion; it's a case where the Marine Corps has no monopoly of interest in what's going on in this room. I ask that the motion be granted.

The veteran lawyer had argued with skill and sincere compassion, but it took young Major Nourie just thirty seconds to dismiss everything he'd just heard:

The motion for opening the hearing to the public is denied.

Motion for dismissal of the charges or, in the alternative, the release of Sergeant Lonetree, is also denied.

Let's take about five minutes, and please be back in place, ready to go. Hearing is in recess.

All of us on the defense team, including military counsel, boiled with rage. Only Clayton remained impassive, perhaps resigned to a lifetime of bad things happening.

But what good did our rage do? We couldn't stand up and pound a table, overturn it, throttle the judge. All we could do was work harder, dig deeper, uncover every questionable aspect of the case, and sooner or later—preferably sooner, for Clayton's sake—bring the matter before the American people.

The Department of State's Kenneth Kidwell was recalled to the stand after the recess, and thirty-one of the thirty-five pages of testimony he gave do not appear in the transcript because they "would damage U.S. national security."

I interrogated Kidwell before he took the stand, as I did every witness, finding the points I felt Kunstler and Stuhff should probe. Typically, my questioning went into greater detail than the lawyers could use in court.

The witnesses in this case, especially the higher-ups due to come later, could be counted on to bridle at having to submit to questions from a professional civilian investigator. They would bring with them slick lawyers from State and CIA, but it didn't matter. I treated them as I would anyone else—all right, maybe rougher, given my increasing conviction that Clayton was being scapegoated.

It would be pointless for me even to condense the several hours of my technical questioning of Kidwell, which formed the basis of his thirty-five pages of testimony. Suffice it to say here that Kidwell talked about the five security disciplines: emanations, the radiation pattern of equipment; physical security; transmission security; and cryptographic security.

None of his testimony remotely connected Clayton Lonetree to the commission of a crime.

Next came the recall of Darrell J. Enderlin.

STUHFF: Gunnery Sergeant Enderlin, what was your duty or your capacity at the Vienna embassy?

ENDERLIN: I was the detachment commander. I was the senior Marine in charge of the Marines at the embassy.

STUHFF: When Sergeant Lonetree was assigned to the Vienna embassy, did you have opportunity to observe his demeanor, attitude, and habits?

ENDERLIN: Yes.

STUHFF: You indicated in one of your statements that you found he was a nice guy and was willing to help, is that correct?

ENDERLIN: He was well liked.

STUHFF: Why was Sergeant Lonetree well liked?

ENDERLIN: Because he wanted to be accepted by other Marines.

STUHFF: On one occasion Sergeant Lonetree confided in you that he was interested in going into the intelligence field, didn't he?

ENDERLIN: Yes. When he first got there.

STUHFF: And you discussed his taking Russian language courses?

ENDERLIN: Yes.

STUHFF: You indicated there was nothing really unusual about his interest in the Russian language. Do you recall making that statement?

ENDERLIN: Yes.

STUHFF: And as far as the Soviet paraphernalia and so forth in his room, was it common practice for Marines on Security Guard duty to acquire such souvenirs when posted?

ENDERLIN: Yes, because they expected eighteen months to two years all over the world, and they pick out things they are interested in. Some people pick up a foreign language. Some just like the way buildings look.

STUHFF: Fire escape plans were kept at the embassy in Vienna, isn't that correct?

ENDERLIN: Correct.

STUHFF: Do you remember where you saw any fire escape plans?

ENDERLIN: By the fire extinguisher or the fire hose itself, and those were located by the elevators.

Stuhff went on to establish that similar floor plans—in plain view of everybody and hardly to be mistaken in importance with, say, the design of a developmental bomber—constituted the secret information Clayton was accused of having passed on to the Russians.

The point stood in stark and painful contrast to all the sensational headlines appearing in newspapers around the world, headlines fed by leaks from self-serving government agencies.

The truth, as it was being revealed inside the Article 32 hearing room, seemed ho-hum indeed. So why, really, did the government want to execute Sergeant Lonetree?

Trying to arrive at my own answer to that increasingly puzzling question, my mind kept coming back to Clayton himself, especially to the remarkable ingenuousness of this young man the government was trying to paint as a spy whose crimes warranted the supreme penalty of death.

Most mornings during the Article 32 hearing, we would meet with Clayton in Major Henderson's small office and discuss the day's strategy. Clayton had a good memory, cooperated willingly, but seldom offered suggestions of his own. He let us make the decisions, as he'd let others make them during his Marine Corps career.

All of us liked Clayton. Nothing about him was hard, cynical, or scheming . . . like the devious nature of a true spy, say a sinister mercenary like John Walker, who for vast sums of money and over almost twenty years severely compromised U.S. security by selling *actual* secrets to the KGB.

Walker and his spy ring truly placed the United States in mortal peril by enabling the Soviets to read all encoded U.S. Navy messages and acquire the most sophisticated American computers.

But the government chose to whitewash Walker's crimes. A Pentagon official told the *Washington Post* that the damage Walker inflicted was "serious but not disastrous." And Sen. David Durenberger, who chairs the Senate Intelligence Committee, said, "I'm not that worried about the information. It certainly wasn't helpful [for it] to end up in Soviet hands, but it wasn't of such significance that there's any kind of alarm."

Author John Barron, who would play an ironic role in Clayton's court-martial, wrote, "It was as if Washington officialdom had been transported to a serene land of fantasy impervious to sinister facts."

Why, in the Walker case, had the government lingered in this land of fantasy? Why the whitewash? Could it be that the full extent of Walker's crimes amounted to such an embarrassment that government officials felt they *had* to play them down? And then, still all too conscious of and smarting from the Walker fiasco, they were delivered an apprehended (actually, self-apprehended) "spy," complete with "confession"—a young Marine on the hottest spot of all, the U.S. Embassy in Moscow. At last, then, a spy in hand, moreover a spy seemingly at the center of what was rapidly becoming yet another government embarrassment: revelations of breached security with who knew how many others—Bracy, for starters—likely to be implicated? Someone must have convinced those at the very top—Weinberger, Reagan—that in Sgt. Clayton Lonetree the government had a chance to redeem its recent embarrassments on the playing fields of the U.S.-Soviet espionage game. We've got him, here's our chance, let's throw the book at him. And so Lonetree would be charged with espionage and would face the death penalty. The same people who had tried to make a molehill out of the mountain of the Walker case were trying to save face by making a mountain out of the molehill of Sgt. Clayton Lonetree, Master Spy.

Well, it was nothing we could prove in the basement of Hochmuth Hall, but it did fill a certain void for me, let's say. And meanwhile, I had the *real* Clayton Lonetree to help and support as I could. I tried to use our morning meetings to get to know him better. He particularly enjoyed reading, and because the brig "library" offered little more than bottom-of-the-line novels, I bent the rules and smuggled books to him.

He asked if I'd bring him a Big Mac, also prohibited. Sure I would. And if the guards sniffed out the contraband, I'd say it was *my* sandwich.

12

A KGB COLONEL NAMED RAYA

April 16, 1987
0805 HOURS

Cpl. John Hlatky was called as a witness for the defense. The
NIS had zeroed in on this spirited Marine guard as a possible
spy—along with another MSG we intended to call, a Cpl. Robert
J. Williams—in the same investigation that had "caught" Bracy.
I had interviewed Hlatky the night before and found him willing
to endanger himself to bring out the truth.

KUNSTLER: With reference to Corporal Williams, have you discussed with him the statements he made?
HLATKY: He didn't elaborate very much, sir. I had a feeling that
some of his statements may have been coerced, or they
weren't completely what he wanted to say.
KUNSTLER: Why did you get that feeling?
HLATKY: He said he wanted to change some of his statements
and he couldn't.
KUNSTLER: Do you know that he indicated, and apparently told
the interrogators, you were engaged in espionage while at
the Moscow embassy?

119

HLATKY: Yes, sir.

KUNSTLER: First of all, was that true?

HLATKY: No, sir, it wasn't.

KUNSTLER: And do you know he said that you were engaged in espionage in return for favors and sex with a Soviet woman?

HLATKY: Yes, sir.

KUNSTLER: Do you remember when you first met Corporal Williams?

HLATKY: Approximately halfway through my tour in Moscow, sir.

KUNSTLER: And from the beginning, did you become good friends with him?

HLATKY: Yes, sir, the first day.

KUNSTLER: With reference to dating a Soviet woman, did you date a Soviet woman?

HLATKY: Yes, sir.

BECK: Mr. Investigating Officer, the witness obviously needs to be warned of his rights under Article 31. He's being asked questions that could very well incriminate him.

Nourie advised the determined Hlatky of his rights against self-incrimination, but this brave, angry Marine wanted to tell his story.

KUNSTLER: Corporal Williams stated that you stayed overnight at the family of the Soviet woman. Was that true?

HLATKY: I stayed at that girl's house, sir.

Hlatky testified that he believed Clayton was a loner, and that the young Marine often took long walks. He accompanied Clayton on one of these to Red Square to watch the changing of the guard.

Hlatky pointed out that at certain times throughout the day, anyone accompanying a small child could come into the embassy. The Marine guards were prohibited from checking their I.D.'s, and obviously a lot of them were Soviets. They would bring the children in and come out themselves alone in the morning, and in the afternoon they would come in alone to pick up the children. They had "free run."

KUNSTLER: Were any attempts made to identify those people or check their I.D.?

HLATKY: We were told not to, sir.

KUNSTLER: Do you know Mr. Mecke?

HLATKY: He was the regional security officer for our embassy, sir.

KUNSTLER: Did Marines have meetings with Mr. Mecke?

HLATKY: Yes, sir. Almost regularly on Friday, sir.

KUNSTLER: Do you recall, at the meetings you attended, were there any complaints made by the Marines about lax security?

HLATKY: I would say almost every week, sir.

KUNSTLER: Can you recall what complaints were made by the Marines to Mr. Mecke with reference to lax security?

HLATKY: Many complaints were made about the cameras, their vantage points, the fact that they were malfunctioning, burned out lights in sensitive areas—the fact about the vehicle gate, sir. The fact that we let Soviets in without checking them if they were picking up their children during those two times a day.

KUNSTLER: Were any of these ever remedied?

HLATKY: Very few of them, sir.

KUNSTLER: Now there was an instance, was there not, with reference to an admiral's wife?

HLATKY: Yes, sir. I was standing Post 1 that day, sir—access control. We had just received word that a certain Soviet individual was not allowed to come back into the embassy.

KUNSTLER: Was that a man or a woman?

HLATKY: It was a female. She was a hairstylist, sir. She had been working with the embassy for over twenty years. The reason for her not being allowed to come back in was she'd been found in areas where she had no reason being. Sometime during my tour that morning, sir, the Admiral's wife brought the lady in for her weekly styling or haircut, sir. I informed her that the Soviet was no longer allowed in the chancery. She sort of gave me a hard time, sir, and asked for the Ambassador's phone number. While I was discussing this with her, a phone was ringing for approximately five or ten rings. So, I picked it up. At which time, she got frustrated and ran in to talk to my detachment commander. The Soviet stayed in front. Later on, I believe the admiral's wife contacted the Ambassador, it went down the chain of command, and the assistant regional security officer came down and cleared her to come in.

Beck cross-examined, mainly to reemphasize that Hlatky had violated a regulation. The Marine made no excuses. He admitted his own fraternizing, and denied emphatically that he had engaged in espionage.

Corporal Hlatky was dismissed from the stand, but a lot more would be heard about him. A loyal Marine proud of his job, like Clayton, he differed from the young Indian defendant mainly by being very aggressive when he saw his government trying to paint him as a traitor. Nor was Hlatky the only one the government was still trying to blame for its own laxity and irresponsiblity.

Corporate Hlatky was never court-martialed. The "spying evidence" against him turned out to amount to zero. Within a few days of his making his statement to the NIS, Corporal Williams, Hlatky's friend, recanted his allegations against Hlatky and against Lonetree, saying he had been pressured and threatened into giving them by government investigators.

We prepared well for the next witness, Fred Mecke of the State Department. I had interviewed Mecke at the State Department in the impressive office of his government attorney.

Mecke sported a goatee and wore an expensive blazer, slacks, and a gold Rolex watch. As expected, he exhibited smoothness, polish, cleverness, and quickness. But we were ready for him. And we had a bombshell of our own to introduce.

STUHFF: You were advised that you were being transferred to Moscow to improve the security at the Moscow embassy?

MECKE: I was advised that I was being transferred to manage the security program at the embassy.

STUHFF: Were there any deficiencies in security procedures in regard to doorways that you considered upon your arrival at Moscow?

MECKE: I considered that there were several entrances that would be better served by new doors, new locks.

STUHFF: Is it correct that the ground level doors inside the court-yard were left unlocked all the time?

MECKE: That is correct.

STUHFF: Did you make any change in regard to that situation?

MECKE: Yes, the equipment was in place by March 1, 1986.

STUHFF: So it took from August of 1985 until March of 1986 for that change to take place?

MECKE: That is correct.

STUHFF: Between that period of August 1985 to March 1986 were those doors locked?

MECKE: No, they were not.

Mecke described Clayton as "quiet," and said that "occasionally on duty he appeared to perform his job in an exceptional manner."

Stuhff hesitated. He was about to place into evidence a photo that would shake the Moscow intelligence community to its foundation.

Operating on experience and a gut hunch, my assistant Mike Wysocki and I had escorted Lonetree, handcuffed, guarded, and in chains, to NIS headquarters at Quantico. We found the photo stored among the young defendant's personal belongings.

At Clayton's request, a friend had taken the picture, and numerous others like it, as mementos of Clayton's tour in Moscow.

STUHFF: Okay, I'm showing you what has been marked for iden-tification as Investigative Exhibit 44, that is a photograph, and I ask if you can identify the persons in that photograph?

MECKE: Uh-hum, on the left is Tom Allen. He is one of the Se-curity Wiring Officers.

STUHFF: Who is the young lady seated next to him?

MECKE: She is a Soviet employee. She worked in the publication procurement office. I don't recall her name.

STUHFF: Does Mr. Allen have his arm around her?

MECKE: She appears to . . . their fingers approach, they may be his.

STUHFF: And she and Mr. Allen are seated on the sofa and having drinks?

MECKE: That is correct.

STUHFF: And there is a gentleman with his arm around two women?

MECKE: That is correct.

STUHFF: The gentleman is wearing a Marine uniform?

MECKE: That is correct.

STUHFF: Who are the two women he is embracing?

MECKE: The two women seated on the couch with him, I do not know the one in the center, but the one on the end is Raya. She worked in the personnel office. She is a Soviet employee.

STUHFF: The Marine. Is that Top Gunnery Sergeant Joe Wingate?

MECKE: It is.

STUHFF: And he has his arms around both those women?

MECKE: I think it is a little clear in this case.

STUHFF: How long has Raya been an employee of the embassy?

MECKE: She had been there for quite a number of years, certainly long before I ever got there.

Raya, identified in John Barron's book, *Breaking the Ring*, as a KGB colonel, handled all travel arrangements for people coming to and leaving the embassy. Thus the KGB knew all U.S. travel plans in and out of Moscow! As Barron revealed, President Reagan was told of Raya's identity, and he ordered her dismissed at once. Only it didn't happen. Raya continued to work for the United States for some time afterward, and in sensitive positions.

So . . . Lonetree guilty of fraternizing? Where were the charges against higher-ups?

Mecke admitted that black-marketeering flourished among various members of the mission, most commonly in currency— the illegal purchase of Soviet money. He told also about the "flea market," an event whereby members of the mission could sell consumer items to other diplomats in Moscow.

STUHFF: And such things would involve everything from Levis to perhaps Rolex watches, such as the one you're wearing?

MECKE: I don't know about Rolex watches, but Levis, certainly.

STUHFF: Were you aware of a report made by a committee headed by Mr. H. Ross Perot into the security of United States missions abroad?

MECKE: I understand there is such a report. I am not familiar with it specifically.

Perhaps he should have been. The new structurally unsound U.S. Embassy (the "old" embassy where Clayton worked was the black-market beehive) had turned into a security nightmare, purportedly riddled with listening devices implanted by the Soviet contractor, a KGB front hired by the U.S. to build the place!

This new embassy, totally compromised by the bungling of high U.S. officials, was a scandal just waiting to explode into headlines.

13

INTERROGATIONS AND CONFESSIONS, NIS STYLE

April 16, 1987
1237 HOURS

The defense began to wonder what case it was trying: the one playing itself out in Hochmuth Hall's basement, with revelations about sloppy security that was no fault of the Marine guards, massive fraternizing at all levels with Soviet nationals, currency speculation, and a black market gone wild; or the one appearing in the press still centered on Clayton Lonetree.

Defense Secretary Weinberger, for instance, was quoted this day as saying: "What is especially revealing about this Soviet intrusion into our embassy . . . is its massive nature. It seems to me to be quite comparable to Iran's actions in seizing our embassy in Tehéran."

To be fair, Weinberger's remark might have had a basis in reality: the Soviets, having built the new embassy (with, as was soon to be charged, built-in listening devices), certainly would have known almost everything that went on inside. But most readers were given to believe that the "massive intrusion" he spoke of became possible because of a few Marine guards, particularly Clayton Lonetree, even though they guarded the *old* embassy.

The defendant himself, as the Article 32 hearing opened its afternoon session, remained passive and accepting of whatever awaited him.

Marine Guard Corporal Robert J. Williams, tall and handsome, opened the afternoon testimony. I knew in advance from questioning him that Williams was outraged by the treatment he had received from the NIS.

Williams testified that Lonetree had told him about Violetta but had mentioned nothing about spying.

"Did you think Clayton's having a Soviet girlfriend was something really horrible?" Henderson asked. "Something nobody else ever did?"

"No, sir."

"Tell us about your first interrogation in April by NIS agents."

"When I got there at seven o'clock in the morning, they started talking to me about Sergeant Lonetree and Bracy, and saying that I wasn't really in trouble."

"Did you have discussions with other Marines who had been interrogated previously by NIS?"

Henderson knew he had. Wysocki and I had gleaned the whole sordid story the previous night.

"Yes, sir," Williams said in a firm voice.

"Did any of them tell you what NIS said about you?"

"Well, they said that, yeah, we really suspect Williams of some misconduct, he is probably with them, with Sergeant Lonetree and Bracy, doing some kind of spying."

"Who was the main interrogator?"

"Well, I had Agent Brannon, and a Ms. Yoker the first two days. She basically sat there playing that Batman and Robin routine with me."

"What are you talking about?"

"Well, sir, they try to play a good cop, bad cop routine, telling me, 'Yeah, you are a good kid. Tell me everything you know about Sergeant Lonetree and Corporal Bracy. You know you didn't do anything—we don't have any suspicions or anything like that— but just tell us everything you know.' "

Henderson did a masterful job guiding Williams through his account of how the NIS obtained statements in this case. Of course the ones we were most concerned about were Clayton's, taken by the very same Thomas Brannon.

"How long were you in there that first day?" Henderson asked Williams.

"From seven o'clock in the morning until about ten o'clock at night."

"Describe the interrogation process."

"They said, 'We don't care about Marines fraternizing. We just want to look at the big picture of everything, the espionage part of it. We don't care about the other stuff that Marines did.' "

"When you were telling them what was going on, how did they respond? How did they act?"

"They would tell me certain things, and if I didn't agree with them, they would kind of get upset. You know, 'Are you sure, are you sure, are you sure, because Lonetree told us that you knew. Bracy even made a statement against you, saying that you told him something in your room.' I said, 'Well, Bracy never told me anything like that.' They would say, 'Yes he did. We got it in a statement. You are lying.' They'd try to do something like that everytime I would say something. They would say, 'You are lying. You're lying. Bracy told you that.' "

"Did they suggest what the proper answer would be?" said Henderson.

"Yes, sir. They were saying, 'Did he ever,'—this is a quote. They said, 'Did he ever mention money to you?', and I said, 'Well, we talked about money, yeah, that is it, we talked about money.' Then they said, 'How much money, thousands of dollars?' I said, 'No, I'm not sure.' 'Yeah, you're sure, come on. Thousands of dollars, like thirty-five thousand dollars?' I said, 'No.' I said, 'Bracy never mentioned money like that.' They asked, 'Did Lonetree ever mention money?' I said, 'No, Lonetree never mentioned any money to me like that.' 'Yeah, you sure? Come on, come on, come on.' "

"Had you been on duty the day before?"

"Yes, sir."

"You were tired?"

"Yes, sir. At first I wasn't tired, but as the day wore on I got pretty worn out."

"Did you ever tell them details they did not put in the statement?"

"Yes, sir."

"Explain that."

"Well, I can't really remember verbatim, but I told things about Bracy, how he didn't tell me certain things. Brannon said, 'He could have done it, and he was approached.' Not that he did, but he was approached. And they kept beating it into me, 'Yeah, he did it,' Mr. Brannon said to me, 'Yeah, you know damn well he did it. You are just trying to cover your ass.' And, I told them, 'Well, I didn't do anything. Do you have charges on me?' He goes, 'No.' I said 'Well, don't try to scare me with that.' And he called other agents into the room. They thought I was going to get violent."

"What was the altercation about?"

"Because he refused to put some of the things in my statement. I went over it again with these new agents, I told them I tried to put things in my statement that they wouldn't put in there. It was just so many things they kept adding that really didn't happen. Like exchange of money, walking around a corner and giving documents over, which never happened. Like Corporal Hlatky putting documents in a bag, like I saw him putting them in a bag, which never happened."

"Corporal Williams, did they actually come up with a written statement for you?"

"Yes, sir. They ran it off on the Wang machine."

"How much time did they give you to look at it?"

"They said, 'Go ahead, sit down and take your time.' And, as I sat down to do that, they were saying, 'Go ahead, read it over.' They gave me enough time, but Mr. Brannon said, 'Come on, Williams, let's go.' He kept talking to me about it."

"Did you tell him about things that you saw that were wrong with that statement?"

"Yes, sir."

"What did they do when you talked to them about things that were wrong in that statement?"

"They said, 'No problem, we'll change it. It's not really important.' "

"Did they agree to make the changes at that time?"

"Yes, sir. They all agreed to make the changes, but they never changed it. They said, 'Nobody will see this. Nobody in the Marine Corps chain of command will see this statement.' They said, 'Only important NIS people. The Marine Corps is not even in the chain of command to see this statement, so don't worry about it.' Then I got into an argument with one of the agents because it said Brasilia, where Corporal Hlatky was. And I asked them why they were sending it to Brasilia, and they go, 'It is not going to Brasilia.' I said, 'Well, I see it right there on the printout.' I said to them 'You're lying, because it's right there. I can see it.' They said, 'No it ain't. Ain't no Marines going to see this. Nobody is going to see it.' "

"Did you sign the statement that night?"

"Yes, sir."

"Why did you sign that statement, knowing it was full of things that didn't happen?"

"Mr. Brannon kept telling me, 'Well, this statement, they are not really going to go by this statement.' He said, 'This is just to clarify a few things and put the puzzle together.' And he said, 'We just need this for our official records.' "

"How much of that statement was information provided to you by the NIS agents?"

"A great deal of it."

"How were you feeling physically at the time you signed that statement?"

"I was tired, sir."

"Did that play any role in your signing the statement?"

"Now that I look back on it, like I told the NIS agents, and I told the prosecutor, I told them I was tired, I just wanted to get out of there, and I shouldn't have signed the statement."

"Let's talk a little bit about that statement specifically. Did you tell the NIS that Bracy had told you about Bracy's espionage activities in Moscow?"

"No, sir. Bracy never mentioned that he was engaged in any espionage. Mr. Brannon is the one who said, 'Well, he must have done something. He must have been involved in it.' "

"Did you ever say anything, or tell the NIS agents anything, about Corporal Hlatky—that Corporal Hlatky was involved in espionage in Moscow?"

"No, sir. They are the ones who added it on, saying, 'Yeah, Corporal Hlatky made a statement already saying that he was involved, and he is already caught.' I said, 'That's impossible because I talked to him just the other day on the phone.' I didn't even think Sergeant Lonetree was engaged in any espionage until it came out in the paper."

"Okay, and you went back the second day. What kind of questions did they ask the second day?"

"At first they just read things off to me. And I asked them, 'Can I see the question?' And they said, 'No.' "

"Did they do the same thing? Were they making suggestions to you again on the second day?"

"When I disagreed with them, they started saying, 'But you told me. You told me. That is what you said.' I said, 'No, that is what *you* said.' And then the whole interview just went downhill after that. Mr. Brannon just got all pissed off, and he is saying that I'm trying to screw him over, that I'm not saying the same things I said the day prior to that."

"What did you tell him?"

"I told him I just wanted to tell the truth. I said to him, 'I don't believe in a lot of the things I said in there. That wasn't what I said; that's what *you* said. I want to change my statement. This is to clarify my first statement, let me clear it up.' "

"Did you actually sign a statement that second time?"

"No, sir. I refused to sign a statement, because the second statement started sounding just like the first statement. Everytime I disagreed with something, they would say, 'No, but you told me that.' Mr. Brannon said, 'I got it in my notes downstairs. You told me so many times.' I said, 'No.' "

Henderson turned the witness over to Major Beck, but before the prosecution's questioning began Nourie issued a warning: "Gentlemen, I have been informed by the Public Affairs Officer that there is a mass of news media out front. I would just remind all parties present that we have a matter of no disclosure of these proceedings to the media."

Nourie should have directed his gag order to those "unidentified sources" who had been painting a dark picture of Lonetree's activities to the press. Better yet: forget it altogether and open the doors so the reporters could hear the testimony depicting government investigators, not the defendant, as the heavies.

Beck asked Corporal Williams, "Did Sergeant Lonetree tell you he was sexually involved with his Soviet girlfriend?"

"No," said Williams. "He just told me that he was involved with her."

"Did you tell Corporal Hlatky anything about NIS coercing you into making statements against him?"

"Yes, sir. I told him that I felt bad, because I told him they were putting words in my mouth, and I said I didn't really say that. The investigators said that."

"Now, according to your sworn statement, you signed a statement saying Bracy told you he was involved in espionage, and that he was paid thousands of dollars for it."

"That is what I was telling you earlier, sir. I told them Bracy never confessed to me that he got money. He confessed to me that he was offered money. He told me he was offered money. The NIS agents were telling me, 'Yeah, he got money.' They kept on saying, 'Yes, yes, he got money, he got money, he got money.' I told them, 'No, he never said he got money.' "

"So, your testimony under oath today is that every time in your sworn statement it says that Bracy told you he was involved in espionage, or Hlatky told you, or you saw that he was involved in espionage, that is completely false?"

"Yes, sir. They wanted me to say things, and we kept on arguing about it and arguing about it. And then they wouldn't let me out of there until I—you know, we started agreeing with what I was saying. I said, 'Okay.' "

Henderson asked Corporal Williams on redirect, "Are you changing your story because Corporal Hlatky was a friend of yours?"

"No, sir," Williams replied.

"Why are you telling a different story from what appears in that statement?"

"Because I was foolish enough to sign a statement just to get out of there. I shouldn't have, to just get out of the people's office.

I thought Corporal Hlatky would take the polygraph test and just pass it. You know, after a while I just said, let me get out of here. That is what I have been feeling bad about. Not bad about Sergeant Lonetree or Corporal Bracy, because it is pretty obvious they did what they did."

"Why is it pretty obvious they did what they did?" asked Henderson.

"Because Mr. Brannon and them people said they made sworn confessions that they did it."

"When you were aware that Hlatky was having an affair or a relationship with a Soviet woman, you knew it was improper, is that true?"

"Yes, sir."

"Why didn't you report it?"

"Because other people were doing it too."

"Other people from where?"

"From the Staff Sergeant all the way to the State Department people."

"Were they having improper relationships with Soviet women?"

"Well, sir, I can't answer, because I have never seen it, but other Marines have told me, so-and-so saw people with Soviet people, like having them over to their house, seeing them with Soviet girls."

"Was it your impression or your feeling at the time you were in the Soviet Union that State Department people were fraternizing with Soviet women?"

"Some of the single people probably have."

The next witness, NIS Special Agent Thomas Brannon, counted as critical to both prosecution and defense. It was he who actually took the incriminating confessions Clayton gave, still the only evidence against our client. We felt, especially after Williams's testimony, that we'd accurately portrayed how much credence should be given such "confessions."

Brannon, five feet eleven inches, perhaps fifty years old, a chain-smoker, had twenty-five years of experience in NIS.

I think he would have liked my assessment of him as a real pro, even though our goals were a hundred and eighty degrees apart. Brannon didn't get emotionally involved. Whether or not Lonetree got off wasn't his concern. He'd had a job to do and he did it, without emotion or anger. Later, after Stuhff tried to cut him down on the witness stand, Brannon said, "I'd have done the same thing in his shoes."

Stuhff asked Brannon if he recalled "telling Sergeant Lonetree at one point during your interrogation to just tell us anything— tell us a lie?"

"No, sir," said the NIS agent. "That is not true. It's out of context."

"When you say that's not true, or that's out of context, you made a statement like that, didn't you?"

"Prior to Sergeant Clayton Lonetree terminating, Clayton Lonetree was talking to me. He told me so many things which he had previously denied, and continued to say different things. I continued to press Lonetree that I believed he had stolen additional secrets which he had not related. I also believe in my mind that he had probably been involved in this activity in Moscow before he came to Vienna."

"What was the foundation for your believing he probably had been engaged in that before?"

"Common sense. Understanding somewhat of the Soviet intelligence system. And the fact that he indicated he was recruited by the Soviets in Moscow and did nothing for them—they paid him money for nothing, and continued to pay him money in Vienna? That just didn't ring correct to me, sir."

"So, you told him, 'Tell us anything; tell us a lie?' "

"He said to me exactly these words, 'Do you want me to lie to you?' and to keep him talking to me, I said, 'Yes, sir.' I said, 'Yes.' I didn't say 'sir.' Yes. He then stated to me that he stole two hundred secrets from the burn bag. The first time he said he also stole two secret binders. I interrupted him and said, 'I bet they were top secret.' I pressed him on that. He acknowledged they were top secret documents and he said he gave them to the Soviets. He also said then 'That is a lie. I didn't do that.' Shortly after that, he asked to seek counsel."

"Special Agent Brannon," Stuhff said, "in the schools you attended, which of them taught this technique of suggesting to a subject that he tell a lie?"

"I did not suggest to him that he tell a lie. He asked me if I wanted him to lie."

"To which, you responded, that indeed is what you were requesting?"

"In essence, that's correct, yes, sir."

After Brannon stepped down, Stuhff turned to another matter.

My persistence had finally succeeded in prying needed evidence out of the government, and now Stuhff came forward to introduce it: "I said when Sergeant Scott was on the stand that I wanted to obtain those logs of Post Number One that indicated people signing out. I've taken the liberty, as you've noticed, of using a green crayon to indicate what you should look through. I've outlined all of Sergeant Lonetree's entries. And I've outlined some others. They are prominent throughout. You'll find bike rides. These are destinations. 'Bike ride,' 'run,' 'PT,' 'practice,' even some from several of the Marines, 'girlfriend's house,' which are in the log. 'Church,' and others besides Sergeant Lonetree, 'walk.' And one of the people who signed out for a walk was Sergeant Scott himself on July twenty-fifth, who wrote down 'walk' as his destination."

So much for Clayton's mysterious "walk" entry, which the prosecution had continually tried to cast in a sinister light. So too, thanks to the candid "girlfriend's house," for any remaining respect for the nonfraternization rules.

But what, after all, had this lengthy Article 32 hearing, about to draw to a close, revealed about the prosecution's case?

The "confessions." That was it. Confessions obtained illegally, with the defendant being urged to lie. Even the government had admitted that some of the confessed "crimes" couldn't have taken place.

The hearing recessed. Closing arguments needed to be prepared. Deep in our bones, we believed we had right, fairness, and justice on our side.

14

PROSECUTION 13, DEFENSE 11

On May 1, ten days before the scheduled final session of the Article 32, the *Washington Post* ran an editorial suggesting a reason, already suspected by the defense, why the government so stubbornly carried on its prosecution of Sergeant Lonetree.

> It would be one thing if, at the conclusion of investigations involving four Marine Embassy Guards, an announcement were to be made that there would be no prosecutions because no violations of law had occurred. But if some unfortunate Pentagon official has to stand up a few weeks from now and announce that there will be no prosecutions because military investigators botched the cases, there will be hell to pay.
>
> Military prosecutors are not commenting. But defense lawyers are not alone in claiming that a number of mistakes have already been made. The whole investigation was begun, after all, not because intelligence agents had uncovered any violations, but rather because Sgt. Clayton Lonetree turned himself in in

Vienna and began to talk. Important decisions were made early and, it has been alleged, without careful consultation with the people who would eventually be responsible for the prosecution.

What kind of warnings were given to these men, and when? Under what conditions were they interrogated? Who decided to offer Cpl. Arnold Bracy immunity (his attorney says it was proffered and refused after three days of interrogation)? And was this proposed deal approved by those ultimately responsible for the investigation? What work has been done—or left undone—to secure evidence that would substantiate statements that some of the accused and some witnesses now seek to retract?

Finally, Who's in charge here? According to news accounts, the Naval Investigative Service is handling the inquiry and the Marines will run the prosecutions. The State Department and the CIA have concerns and responsibilities. And the Justice Department and the FBI are, for the moment, standing aside until it is determined whether the cases will be brought in military or in civil criminal courts. One Marine Corps memo obtained by the "MacNeil/Lehrer Newshour" suggests that a multi-agency task force would be a good idea to "put some distance between us and the investigation. prosecution." Translation: spread the blame.

If the cases involving the Marine Security Guards fall apart for any reason other than the innocence of those involved, it will be a second scandal.

The either/or implicit in the last paragraph didn't apply in the Lonetree case. Yes, the government had bungled the situation. But, also, yes, the government didn't have the necessary evidence against Clayton. From the standpoint of the authorities, it seemed to us that the best move would be to dismiss all charges for lack of evidence, and hope the bungling remained below the surface.

May 11, 1987
0903 H O U R S

The media ban was still in force, but that didn't keep me from wishing the whole world could hear Kunstler arguing the defense motion to dismiss charges.

"We know," Kunstler summarized, "that failure to corroborate a statement alleged to be made by an accused means the statement cannot be introduced into evidence, and therefore there is essentially no evidence against Sergeant Lonetree.

"There isn't," he continued, "a shred of corroborative testimony before you with reference to Lonetree's statement. I have attended all of these hearings but one, and I have heard nothing. I have checked with co-counsel, and it is their opinion there is nothing that corroborates and gives an inference of truth to the statements attributed to Sergeant Lonetree."

Kunstler went on to argue that dismissal was even in the prosecution's best interest (underlying his points was the Marine Corps' own increasingly evident dissatisfaction with the case, particularly as handled, virtually from the start, by the NIS):

"It does the Marine Corps no good. Our position here: this is the wrong defendant. The State Department should be here, and not Sergeant Lonetree. The Marine Corps is as much a defendant in this case as Sergeant Lonetree, and neither one should be a defendant here.

"We don't think it is right and proper and moral to keep Sergeant Lonetree, who has been in the brig now as you know for over four months, while Lieutenant Colonel Oliver North walks free, suspected of charges of the most serious nature involving the violation of Congressional dictates."

Next Kunstler talked about selective prosecution, that is, trying an individual on charges overlooked in other cases.

Before going to the close, the defense called one last witness, Kenneth J. Kelliher, to give the board one final example of the constitutionally illegal, let alone unethical, methods of interrogation and "confession" on which the government's case was based. Sergeant Kelliher had been with the MSG Battalion for three years, posted in Moscow and Bern, Switzerland. Although he'd known nothing about the charges against Clayton or Corporal Bracy, the NIS had interrogated him for fourteen days.

"What kind of threats did they make?" Henderson asked.

"I can't recall it word for word," Kelliher said, "but something along the line that if I didn't pass the polygraph, I wouldn't be able to go home, I would . . . imprisonment."

"But you were going to prison if you didn't pass the polygraph?"

"Yes, that was my understanding."

"Did they make any threats concerning your girlfriend from Switzerland?"

"Yes, again, if I didn't pass the polygraph, she would not be allowed to come to our country." NIS had threatened that even if Kelliher were to marry his Swiss girlfriend, she would be sent back to her country.

On the last day of his interrogation, an NIS agent called him an asshole, picked up a stack of pens and markers, and threw them against the door in a burst of anger.

After Kelliher, another MSG guilty of no crime whom the NIS had tried to bully into making accusations against others, was dismissed, only the closing arguments remained to complete the Article 32.

NOURIE: As I understand it, the defense wishes to have two individuals make arguments, that being Mr. Stuhff and Major Henderson, is that correct?

STUHFF: That is correct.

NOURIE: I would like to hear from the government first, if they have any statements they wish to make.

BECK: The government has no statements to make, Mr. Investigating Officer.

There were two possible explanations for Beck's refusal to deliver a closing statement. Either he was brimming with confidence on the strength of his case, a confidence the defense believed unwarranted, or he knew something we didn't, namely that it didn't matter what had been said or proved: Sgt. Clayton Lonetree was headed for a court-martial with his life at stake.

The defense couldn't assume anything. It had to do its best and then just hope for victory. Stuhff rose to deliver one of the most important closing arguments of his career. I thought he did an outstanding job. He showed the confessions had been illegally obtained, and that the required-by-law corroboration was totally absent.

Henderson spoke next. He knew military law inside out, and if Nourie was disinclined to agree with the civilian Stuhff, maybe the words of a fellow officer would move him toward a just recommendation.

Nourie closed the Article 32 investigation, and would make his report to Gen. Frank E. Petersen, Commander of Quantico.

There was nothing left for Sergeant Lonetree and his defense team but to await General Petersen's ruling.

Prosecution 13, Defense 11. That's how the headline would have read if Clayton's Article 32 ordeal had been a sports contest. On May 16, 1987, four days after the Article 32 hearing closed, Quantico's Commanding Gen. Frank E. Petersen ruled that eleven of twenty-four charges against Lonetree be dropped, including the ludicrous accusation that he allowed Soviet agents to roam freely through the embassy during "moonlight tours."

It was, everyone assured the defense, "a great victory." We weren't so sure. Once committed to prosecution, the military historically did not back down, no matter how wrongheaded the charges might be.

At least one of General Petersen's rulings classified as a defense victory, and a major one at that: Clayton could no longer receive the death penalty.

Thankful for small favors—could a court-martial panel, subject to pressure from the highest levels of government, have been counted on *not* to execute Clayton?—the defense nonetheless remained appalled by the sentence the Native American could still receive: dishonorable discharge, loss of all pay and allowances, reduction to the lowest enlisted pay grade, and life imprisonment.

Even the charges that were dropped got thrown out gracelessly. Clayton didn't face the "moonlight tours" accusation, an official

Marine Corps statement read, because the evidence "consists principally of hearsay which is not admissable at trial."

But "hearsay" could be true. The statement implied that Clayton *might* be guilty but had beaten the rap because of "hearsay evidence," a technicality. In truth, the "hearsay evidence" consisted of Corporal Bracy's "statement," which (unbeknownst at that time to the defense) had been declared false for being obtained by altering the results of polygraph tests.

Nor could Lonetree take much heart from the dropping of eleven charges. As a Marine official pointed out to us, "There is still an ongoing criminal investigation," adding that Clayton still "could be prosecuted for these offenses if the evidence justifies the charges."

Every charge stemming from Clayton's "statements" after Brannon urged him to lie had been dropped. This represented a double-edged sword: it cut against the prosecution because the charges had been thrown out, but it also cut against Clayton because now any judge could be counted on to rule that Brannon's self-defeating remarks could not be admitted in evidence.

On June 12, 1987—one month after the closing of the Article 32 hearing, and with the convening of the Lonetree court-martial still a month away—the government dropped all charges against Cpl. Arnold Bracy (except the charge of fraternization, even though Bracy, whose fundamentalist religion forbade premarital sex, had reported to authorities the sexual advances of the Soviet woman with whom he was accused of fraternizing; although Bracy was never prosecuted on the charge, the NIS clearly felt it had to keep something pending on this innocent Marine to justify its draconian efforts to discredit him).

NIS agents, it came out, had changed the results of lie-detector tests administered to Bracy, including his denial of conspiracy with Clayton!

Hooked up to a polygraph machine, Bracy answered no to these questions: "Has anyone ever asked you to engage in espionage against the United States?" And, "Have you ever engaged in espionage against the United States?"

The polygraph machine showed "no deception indicated." The NIS agents who interrogated Bracy reported the readings accurately, but NIS *headquarters* ordered them to change the readings to "deception indicated."

No one in NIS headquarters has ever been indicted, though here was the one real crime in this whole sordid episode. At the end of Bracy's months-long nightmare, his Marine Corps lawyer, Lt. Col. Michael Powell, stated: "Corporal Bracy is innocent not because of any technicality or lack of evidence. He is innocent because the things they said he did didn't occur. They did not happen. They were fantasy in the minds of NIS agents. Fantasy."

Bracy's exposure of NIS investigative and interrogative conduct came a month too late for Clayton's Article 32 hearing—during which, unquestionably, the government leaks exercised considerable damage to public opinion of Lonetree—but at least now continuing government statements on the "Moscow spy scandal" were received by the press with growing skepticism.

June 16, 1987
THE WASHINGTON POST

The espionage cases against Marine Guards at the U.S. Embassy in Moscow have begun to fall apart. There are two possible explanations. Either the original charges were blown out of all proportion and no serious offenses occurred, or a serious case was mishandled by investigators and now a prosecution is impossible. In either case there appears to have been a terrible bungle, and an explanation is owed the public.

All 28 guards at the Moscow embassy were ordered home in April. This was, of course, a heck of a story involving, as it did, international intrigue, spies, sex and an elite corps of young military men. Cabinet members and other high government officials expressed outrage and hinted of irreparable damage to the security of the western world. Members of Congress denounced the American ambassador and the

Moscow embassy staff of a horrendous failure to maintain security, and called for their punishment.

Then gradually, the story began to unravel. The most serious charges against Sgt. Lonetree—that he had allowed Soviets inside the embassy—have been dropped. Those stemming from his own confession that he had been involved with a woman are still pending. . . . Cpl. Bracy recanted his confession, saying it had been coerced. In the absence of any physical evidence at all to substantiate the confession, the Marines have now dropped the charges against Cpl. Bracy and released him from custody.

What's going on? Is there a major scandal here or not? Are we left with two cases of young Marines who in the end will be charged only with having Russian girlfriends? Was there or wasn't there a real breach of security at the embassy? Were KGB agents inside the building at all? And if all of this did happen but no prosecutions can be brought, what happened during the investigation that sabotaged the cases? The slow sorting out, the trickling away of charges won't do. The Pentagon must explain what has happened and why. The public, the young men involved, and the Marine Corps deserve no less.

The *Post* had more questions to ask in another June 16 article, where it zeroed in on the Defense Department and NIS. Reading the piece and realizing that the paper was on the right track, I could only wish that they had been allowed to witness the flimsy government case presented at Lonetree's Article 32 hearing:

For weeks little doubt has been expressed by Defense Secretary Caspar Weinberger or other top administration officials about the damage that Marine Guards caused at the U.S. Embassy in Moscow.

The United States has suffered "a very great loss," Weinberger said in a March 28 interview on Cable News Network, the day two guards were accused of allowing Soviet intelligence agents into the building. On April 16, he attacked the Soviets for running "a massive espionage campaign" that extended into "some of the most sensitive rooms in our embassy in Moscow."

Last Friday, after the Marine Corps dropped all charges against the second Embassy Guard implicated in the case, it was clear that the government would have difficulty proving the case that Weinberger and other administration officials were making a few weeks earlier. Cpl. Arnold Bracy, the accused Marine, and his lawyers said it simply: The alleged embassy entries did not occur.

Defense Department spokesmen said yesterday that Weinberger stood behind his statement and that the Soviet incursions were "a matter of record." His rhetoric was not overstated, a spokesman said.

What may have happened, said defense lawyer Lt. Col. Michael L. Powell, was a "fantasy" created by members of the Naval Investigative Service (NIS), the largely civilian police force within the Navy Department charged with investigating crimes by members of the Navy and Marine Corps.

Lawyers for Sgt. Clayton J. Lonetree, the first Marine charged, had made similar claims since Lonetree's arrest. But because Lonetree remains jailed on espionage charges based on his own statement, his credibility may have seemed in question.

Bracy, 21, was cleared of all charges. Yesterday, on ABC-TV's "Good Morning America," he repeated his contention that NIS agents tricked him during interrogation.

Moreover, as Bracy's lawyers have pointed out, he is not alone in making such statements. Not only has Lonetree made such allegations, but at least three other former Moscow embassy guards who testified at Bracy's pretrial hearings said that NIS agents attempted to threaten them and get them to sign false statements.

As in Bracy's case, many were taken off-base to a nearby motel where they were questioned for hours, often while hooked up to polygraph machines, and were told that a statement was the only way out. It was part of a worldwide NIS investigation that involved more than 100 agents and was code named Cabin Boy.

"I don't like to say, 'I told you so,' but I did," said Rep. Jim Bates (D-Calif.), who for years has argued that the Naval Investigative Service is inept. "It continues to fumble and bungle the major issues given to it," he said.

Then, none other than Clayton's favorite author, John Barron, revealed in the June *Reader's Digest* some of the security problems being encountered in the Soviet Union:

The new U.S. Embassy in Moscow, scheduled for completion in 1983, was meant to be a symbol and showplace of America. But when Senate investigators inspected the unfinished building last fall, they could scarcely believe what they saw.

The roof of the eight-story structure leaked so badly that puddles stood on the fourth floor and water dripped down the elevator shafts to the basement. Holes and gaps pocked the interior walls. Chunks of concrete had fallen off ceilings. Outside, seepage stained the facade and cracked its mortar.

Worse, American security officers found the building riddled with sophisticated listening devices. One steel girder turned out to be, in effect, a giant antenna. Hundreds of other interrelated devices embedded in the columns, beams and floors made the entire building the equivalent of a microphone, capable of relaying to KGB listeners the softest whispers. Beneath the embassy, security men discovered that the Soviets had dug tunnels that could be used for surreptitious entry into the American compound or for housing more spy equipment.

It made me think . . . if the government was truly concerned about losing secrets, it should have launched vigorous open investigations into the building of the new Moscow embassy and perhaps handed down some indictments. But, of course, that would have required looking into the actions of high State Department officials, who had hired the KGB contractors in the first place. Safer to rest the whole mess on a lone Indian noncom, the only card they had left, and hope that the result of his court-martial would leave him with enough blame to satisfy the eyes and conscience of the public.

PART THREE

Court-Martial

15

BIG JOHN AND LITTLE JOHN

The court-martial opened on June 22, 1987, in a large room on the first floor of base headquarters at Quantico, Military Judge Capt. Philip Roberts presiding.

Judge Roberts, a jovial and portly man, confided that he'd handled four thousand cases in the past ten years, an awesome total. Smiling broadly, he could switch easily from Jekyll to Hyde. During the court-martial Roberts always had a "Nice day, isn't it?" greeting for defense team members in the hallway, and a "Motion denied" in the courtroom.

"Is it true," a reporter later asked Kunstler, "that Judge Roberts has denied every defense motion?"

"Absolutely not," Kunstler said. "He's granted every motion for a recess that we've asked for."

Ten to fifteen spectators could fit into the room, and more of the curious viewed the proceedings via closed-circuit television in another room down the hall. The press itself (with the exception of a sketch artist) was allowed in neither room. Instead, the fourth estate watched closed-circuit television in a nearby house atop a small hill. Whenever "national security" matters came up, which was often, guards cleared the two rooms at base headquarters and all TV coverage ceased. Under this system, the press had an understandably difficult time gathering news. One minute they were following the drama, the next they were staring at a blank screen.

Three of the seats in the court-martial room were the total set aside for Clayton's supporters. Sally Tsosie and her sister, Mae Benally, attended frequently, and Spencer and Craig Lonetree came on other occasions. The venerable Sam Lonetree showed up once. Other seats were allotted to "observer" lawyers representing the CIA, NIS, and State Department, and the simply curious were left lucky to grab one or two.

The court-martial panel consisted of ten officers. They were equivalent to a civilian jury, except that they decided both guilt or innocence and the penalty. The panel did not attend the opening sessions. These were set aside to argue defense motions to suppress Clayton's "confessions." Realistically, the defense expected the probable outcome of the trial to ride on Judge Roberts's decision. If the judge ruled the confessions inadmissible, the prosecution's case went out the window. If he allowed the confessions, the defense would be reduced mainly to finding error in the court-martial for use in a later appeal.

But even if admitted, the confessions would require corroboration. The defense didn't believe the prosecution had such corroboration, not with the entire case against Clayton based on his own statements rather than investigative work by the government. Still, we were inclined to suspect—correctly, as it turned out—that the other side would introduce something or someone to satisfy Judge Roberts.

The charges against Clayton, which because of repetition of the same accusations seemed to amount to more than they actually numbered, boiled down to this:

1. Clayton gathered names and photographs of covert agents, and turned them over to Sasha.
2. Clayton had meetings with Violetta, Sasha, and George.
3. Clayton failed to report telephonic and personal contacts with Sasha and Violetta while in Moscow.

4. The same as Number 3, for Sasha in Vienna, plus contact by mail.
5. Clayton identified covert agents for Sasha.
6. Clayton discussed "national defense information" with Sasha and Violetta, and "did agree to obtain, or attempt to obtain, floor plans to the United States Embassy, Moscow."
7. Clayton wrongfully revealed to Sasha the "identities, addresses, and phone numbers" of covert agents.
8. Clayton secreted a list of covert agents in his room.

The following, point-by-point, represents the defense's assessment of the charges:

1. Yes, Clayton gave three photos to Sasha. Two were of agents already transferred, and *all* the covert agents were already known to the Soviets. Clayton turned the pictures over figuring them harmless, and believing in his double-agent-obsessed mind that they might help him help the U.S. Certainly he made a mistake in judgment, but no damage was done.
2. Yes, Clayton had meetings with Violetta, Sasha, and George. Basically, this was a fraternization offense, and from our Article 32 experience we were confident we'd be able to show that hardly *anyone* in the Moscow or Vienna embassies remained free of this taint.
3. "Failure to report" contacts. Okay. But hardly a major offense. And eventually he *did* report them.
4. The "mail contact" involved love letters from Violetta.
5. This offense involved pairing the right husband with the right wife. They were photos Sasha had. Lonetree had not brought them to the Soviets.
6. The "national defense information" Clayton and Sasha discussed involved conversation any two people might have about, say, U.S. and Soviet policy in the Middle East. Clayton gave away no secrets. He did not give away actual floor plans to the embassy in Moscow. He had stalled Sasha on that, knowing he'd soon leave Moscow.
7. As for "identities, addresses, and phone numbers" of covert agents, Clayton had simply turned over an unclassified embassy phone book easily accessible to anyone.

8. Possession of a list of covert agents is no crime. And as the prosecution itself allowed, Clayton didn't turn his list over to Sasha or anyone else. In short, this "crime" wasn't a crime.

So much for the government case. So much for all the outcry, the worldwide headlines, the dire emanations from Secretary Weinberger and other high government officials right up to President Reagan. Where was the beef? Nor could we find consolation in the fact that Clayton "only" faced life imprisonment. What he should have faced, at the most, was a dishonorable discharge from the Corps.

The prosecution began its argument against our motions to suppress the confessions by asserting that only police agencies, whether military or civilian, have to give Miranda warnings.

The defense said Baloney, the CIA may be chartered as an intelligence-gathering apparatus rather than a police agency, but if it looks like a duck, walks like a duck, and quacks like a duck, then . . .

Also, we argued that the CIA, through "Harold Johnson" and "Charles Trunk," got what it could from Clayton, then turned the information over to the NIS team. Thus, in reality, the CIA, the NIS, and all the other agencies involved formed an "indivisible entity" which in effect conspired to deny Clayton his fundamental constitutional rights.

The first witness to testify, referred to earlier in this book as Harold Johnson, became known officially as Big John for purposes of the court-martial record.

Why "Big John?" Court participants needed a handle for the witness, and the CIA refused to allow his real name.

Just as the Article 32 had marked time with a long wrangle over security clearances, the court-martial opened with a tug of war over the witness's identity. William Kunstler suggested "Big Bathroom," and that the second witness—"Charles Trunk"—be dubbed "Little Bathroom." Judge Roberts finally settled on Big John and Little John.

BECK: Did you, on 14 or 15 December, advise the accused of any kind of Miranda or Article 31 rights?

BIG JOHN: No.

BECK: And why is that?

BIG JOHN: Well, I really wouldn't have been familiar with what those rights were specifically, and I was viewing this as a counterintelligence matter. I was not even thinking in those kinds of terms.

He wasn't? Surely this veteran agent knew he would be turning over everything he'd learned to NIS.

Mike Stuhff soon took over the questioning.

STUHFF: But you knew Sergeant Lonetree was going to be debriefed or interrogated, or whatever term you want to use, by a subordinate of yours. That was set up on the 15th?

BIG JOHN: Yes. I would characterize it as a debriefing.

STUHFF: And you knew the subordinate was going to question him on the possibility of the commission of espionage?

BIG JOHN: Yes.

STUHFF: And you knew it's a crime for American citizens to engage in espionage with a foreign country?

BIG JOHN: Yes, if I think about it, I certainly recognize that espionage is a crime.

STUHFF: Right. And you also knew, did you not, that after you were through with him, with this debriefing, that if any criminal actions were revealed, that you were going to turn it over to the proper authorities, weren't you?

BIG JOHN: [The answer is missing from the court-martial transcript.]

It should not be missing from this book. Big John answered, "Yes," he intended to turn his information over to prosecutors.

Next came Little John, called Charles Trunk earlier in this account. He was the man who had been introduced to Clayton by Big John at the McDonald's in Vienna.

To our surprise, Little John came across as a babbling fount of information. He admitted to speaking "French, Russian, Spanish, a little bit of Serbo-Croatian, and German." No, he hadn't thought to advise Clayton of his rights against self-incrimination.

BECK: Did you advise the accused of any rights, commonly referred to as Miranda or Article 31?

LITTLE JOHN: No, I did not.

BECK: And why?

LITTLE JOHN: Because I was not arresting him or gathering information for a trial, or exercising any other law enforcement responsibility.

Of course he was gathering information for a trial. This one! Yet, the fact that he intended to let NIS, fully briefed by him, bring the information to the prosecutors of this very trial didn't seem to matter to its presiding judge.

The prosecution and defense elicited from Little John the same information Clayton had given in his accounts to me. The question was, did the CIA qualify as a police agency? (The very mention of the agency's name was classed as a secret and forbidden during the court-martial. Talking to the press, we of the defense had to use the phrase "certain intelligence agency" to make our point.)

STUHFF: And were you aware at the time that espionage can possibly be punished by death?

LITTLE JOHN: Yes, sir.

STUHFF: And of course you never told Sergeant Lonetree that the information which you were obtaining from him was being shared with the Naval Investigative Service?

LITTLE JOHN: No, sir.

The aura of secrecy and cover-up that seemed to permeate Clayton's trial from the start, amounting at times to paranoia, was brought home to me by something that happened soon after Little John was excused.

The defense was naturally curious about the court-martial watchers, and one spectator in particular caught my eye. She stood five feet six inches and approached two hundred pounds, was dressed primly, like a matron, but had the face of an angel.

"I'm Lake Headley, investigator for the Lonetree defense."

"Yeah."

"Would you mind identifying yourself?

"I'm Angelique White. I'm the Lonetree case agent for the NIS."

"I'm looking forward to interviewing you."

"I don't think that interview will happen."

But I did interview Angelique White, in Henderson's office in the headquarters building. Right at the start she pulled out a tape recorder.

"In other interviews," I said, "taping hasn't been allowed."

"I don't know about your other interviews, but I'm taping this one or there won't be an interview."

"Okay. I'll get my tape recorder from the other room."

"Why bother? We'll provide the defense with a copy."

"Okay."

I wasn't about to start an argument about any such "copy," but after asking some basic personal questions for about twenty minutes—name, age, background—I went to fetch a cup of coffee and came back with my own tape recorder.

"Why'd you get that?" Ms. White wanted to know.

"Well, I'd like to get this right. Two are better than one. These things break down."

"You don't need it. I promise I'll give you a copy."

How could I mistrust Angelique? But I did, and taped the rest of the interview. The next day I approached the NIS agent: "Angelique, let me have your transcript. I need those first twenty minutes."

"There isn't going to be any transcript."

"What do you mean? I got your promise."

"I know what I promised. That's changed. I've been ordered not to provide you with a transcript."

"I thought you more professional than that."

"I don't care about your personal opinions. And I've been instructed to tell you to turn over your tapes to Sergeant Lugo. Those tapes are classified."

Lugo was in charge of courtroom security.

"What are you people afraid of?" I asked.

"I'm not going to debate with you, Mr. Headley," Ms. White said huffily, turning to walk away. "That's the final word."

But it wasn't.

Sergeant Lugo, who turned out to be open-minded throughout

the court-martial, soon approached me and asked for the tape. "I've got to pick it up," he said almost apologetically.

Stuhff soon obtained a court order to have the tape returned. I couldn't help gloating when Angelique White asked me petulantly, "When do you want it?"

Defense and prosecution had had their innings with NIS Agent David Moyer at the Article 32, and with Kunstler questioning, Major Roberts got to hear, as had Captain Nourie at the hearing, of the "tell us a lie, tell us anything" urgings of Thomas Brannon. Kunstler elicited an additional nugget:

KUNSTLER: With reference to Sergeant Lonetree, did you come to the opinion at any time that he was fabricating things to increase incriminatory statements, making it look like he was more guilty than he was?

MOYER: I think in several areas the sergeant was fabricating, perhaps embellishing some areas, and reducing his culpability in still additional areas.

KUNSTLER: Well, didn't you think at one time that he was fabricating and increasing his culpability?

MOYER: Yes, sir.

Another wearer of blazer and slacks, Gary Hardgrove, had been one of the NIS agents to whom Little John transferred Clayton.

Hardgrove's basic testimony backed up David Moyer's: the NIS had faithfully and daily informed Clayton of his rights, and the young Indian talked on and on. The fact that Lonetree was living in a motel room in England at the time, believing, among other things, that he was interviewing for a double-agent job, seemed immaterial· to Hardgrove.

Capt. Andy Strotman questioned Hardgrove for the defense, and adroitly brought out that the decision to arrest Lonetree had been made while Little John was still questioning Clayton. And of course, these agents of the CIA (who couldn't even be named, let alone CIA-identified at the court-martial) had not read Lonetree his rights before passing his admissions along to the NIS. All of which was patently illegal, but would count so only if the court held Big John and Little John to have been working for a police agency. In that case, all the "evidence" subsequently acquired would be considered tainted and ruled inadmissible.

Next came Thomas Brannon. Stuhff cut quickly to the point with this NIS agent/polygraph operator/interrogator who had urged Clayton to lie.

STUHFF: Generally what you try to do is remove the suspect from his own office quarter or from his own home for the interrogation to take place over some period of time?
BRANNON: That would be correct.
STUHFF: And one of the things that you did very effectively, when you pressed Sergeant Lonetree and argued with him, is you got him to confirm your belief that he was guilty?
BRANNON: That was the end result, Mr. Stuhff.
STUHFF: Because when you came in to interview him on the 28th of December at two o'clock, your supervisors had told you they believed he was guilty?
BRANNON: Yes, sir, they questioned the veracity of his denials.
STUHFF: And you kept telling Sergeant Lonetree what you thought the truth was?
BRANNON: I didn't know what the truth was. I had ideas, thoughts, some of which I expressed, many of which were expressed by him.

Harry Sperber followed Brannon. This NIS dress-alike agent testified only briefly, the defense bringing out again that Clayton had been placed under arrest without realizing it.

Sperber's was the last testimony of the portion of the court-martial devoted to suppression hearings.

16

ROBERTS'S RULES

"I want to introduce you to General Petersen," Kunstler said to me as we stood at a coffee machine during the lunch hour.

"Sure you do."

Kunstler enjoyed practical jokes, and this surely ranked as one. Quantico Commanding Gen. Frank Petersen was the convening authority for Clayton's court-martial, and although he had dropped eleven of the twenty-four charges at the conclusion of the Article 32 hearing, and had removed the possibility of the death sentence, I hardly considered him a friend of the defense.

"I'm serious," Kunstler said. "He wants to meet you. Come on. He's in the barber shop."

The much-decorated black general was indeed in a barber chair, from which he rose to greet me with a warm smile and firm hand.

"I was a youngster in Topeka, Kansas," General Petersen said, "when Mr. Kunstler came to my school and talked about Brown. He's one of my gods."

The Brown the general referred was Linda Brown of *Brown v. the Board of Education of Topeka*, one of the nation's landmark civil rights cases. The respect General Petersen held for Kunstler, whom he had listened to as a black schoolboy three and a half decades ago, gleamed on his face.

"How is the case going?" Petersen asked.

He knew very well how the case was progressing. "Your guards say my hair is too long," I answered.

"Lake, your hair is just perfect," Petersen said.

Later I thought about the irony of that meeting . . . the fate of Kunstler's client in this major case being largely in the hands of a man who had listened to the civil rights lawyer as a black school child that long-past day, his chances of becoming, say, a Marine Corps general boosted by the landmark case Kunstler himself had lectured about.

In a sense, I knew, the Marine Corps didn't stand as a major villain here. In fact, the case embarrassed the Corps. Someone as astute as Petersen had to know that.

The Marine Corps, specifically the Moscow Marine Guards, had been scapegoated. *All* had been relieved of their Soviet posts. And, more specifically, Marine Sgt. Clayton Lonetree had been scapegoated to protect the higher ranking civilians actually responsible for the embassy fiasco.

I didn't need Kunstler to tell me that Petersen loved the Marine Corps. You aren't promoted to general if you don't. Seeing what was going on must have cut him to the quick.

And not just General Petersen. Especially sympathetic to Clayton throughout the ordeal were the Marine guards he worked with in Moscow. They remembered him as quiet, pleasant, eager to help out—hardly a potential spy. And of course—when push came to shove—they saw first-hand how the NIS tried to implicate *them.*

The first two motions by the defense, argued by Maj. David Henderson, contended that a fair trial for Clayton had become impossible due to the long, continuing barrage of newspaper and TV stories prompted by government leaks and bearing no relation to the legal proceedings; also that "command influence"—the statements of Caspar Weinberger and many other high-ranking officials—would inevitably exercise an irresistible influence on the members called upon to reach a verdict. These members, whose ultimate boss was Caspar Weinberger, Secretary of Defense, would need to possess courage and character beyond that of most mortal men to go against the person who held their careers in his hand. Major Henderson quoted Upton Sinclair: "It is difficult to get a man to understand something when his salary depends on his not understanding it."

Military Judge Roberts, he of the smile in the hallway, ruled against both defense motions.

About a fair trial being impossible because of the press coverage, Roberts ruled that officials "are permitted to acknowledge the existence of potential offenses," and "there was no expressed belief in the guilt of the accused." Weinberger's calling for Clayton's execution was "predicated upon a proper finding of guilt," and besides, "The Secretary of Defense does not have control over which of his comments may go into bold type."

About command influence, our contention that court members knew what verdict their superiors wanted, Roberts said:

> If a comment that the Secretary of Defense believes that a severe punishment is appropriate was made, as it appears it was, then defense will have an opportunity to find out if anybody at the level of court member was influenced by this. This, however, is not command influence per se, inasmuch as these were comments made far removed from the trial level, and not addressed to anyone in particular but basically responses to press inquiries concerning the thoughts and feelings of the Secretary of Defense.

The several days required to argue these defense motions were unhappy ones for us. We had all given maximum effort over a period of months for a case we felt strongly about, but nothing we had to say seemed to make any impression on the military judge. The formal court-martial hadn't yet started, but I felt his mind was already made up.

Henderson next argued that the prosecution hadn't complied with the ninety-day "speedy trial" requirements of the UCMJ.

Roberts ruled against us. He said the delays were "unavoidable."

How were they unavoidable? The case had run over the ninety-day limit because of the government's initial refusal to give clearances to the defense team, and because at the twelfth hour the prosecution had reset the clock with a new set of charges, all of which had been long since disproved.

I thought Roberts's rulings outrageous. So did the others on the defense team. Only Clayton, sitting quietly at the defense table alone with his thoughts, refrained from expressing what he felt.

The small courtroom, packed with its dozen spectators, tensed to hear Kunstler argue the motion to dismiss the charges because of NIS misconduct. The wily warrior took aim and fired both barrels, the first at Agent Thomas Brannon, "who testified before you with that horrifying statement to tell a suspect, 'tell us anything, tell us lies,' to encourage fantasy so that you could fill out a case."

Kunstler went on: "Sergeant Kelliher, who is on Page 396, told a graphic story of being questioned for over fourteen days at the Washington Naval Yard, and of being told that unless he came across and incriminated Sergeant Lonetree or Corporal Bracy, or both of them, that he would be prosecuted himself, that his Swiss girlfriend would not be allowed to come into the country, that he would be drummed out of the Marine Corps.

"You have Corporal Williams at Page 312. You have Sergeant Kelliher at 396. And you already can take judicial notice of this infamous Bracy episode.

"These circumstances, the fabrication of material, the threats, the terrorization of young men, who are ones who would be vulnerable to a chain of command or what they thought to be a chain of command investigation, the continuous and relentless interrogation, the salting away in these hotel rooms, the threats, the furnishing of misleading information to Corporal Bracy, telling him in essence that Sergeant Lonetree had confessed to all the crimes and, therefore, all they needed from him was to fill in so they could get a better case in court, these are all despicable things."

Judge Roberts ruled:

> I expect it's safe to say that the court and the government do not favor or condone the types of tactics that were recited by the defense. I assume in situations where the defense is aware that the court dismissed charges in what was labeled as a therapeutic dismissal, that the misconduct at issue was misconduct in that case, and not the misconduct of other individuals in other cases. The court, however, believes that there is no evidence before the court today that would make other witnesses' testimony relevant to this trial. Accordingly, the motion to dismiss for NIS misconduct is denied.

Finally, and most importantly, Kunstler and Stuhff, citing multiple precedents, argued that Clayton's confessions should be suppressed.

Stuhff brought out some of the most important reasons why the confessions should get thrown out:

> In the Kellam Case, one of the more recent cases, which discusses the scope of Article 31, a deputy sheriff, who was not an employee of the United States Government, was involved. That deputy sheriff was allowed by Air Force authorities to assume a role. And it was found in Kellam that that was not proper.
>
> The Swift Case, one of the landmark cases, the seminal case, set forth the principle that if two agencies—usually both are police agencies—merge into an indivisible entity, then any member of either agency must advise a suspect of his rights under Article 31, under Miranda, under Tempia.
>
> There was as well unlawful inducement, as that term is defined, and is defined in the military cases, for Ser-

geant Lonetree to make the statements he made to Little John.

I think the primary case for the court to look at in this regard is Whipple. In Whipple, a seaman on board ship was induced to make application for a so-called drug exemption program. He approached the drug exemption officer, handed the drug exemption officer a sack, which contained a quantity of cocaine, made an incriminating confession about his possession of that drug, and made application to become a participant in a publicized drug exemption program, in which he was not promised immunity, but it was implied to him that he would receive some benefit, some reward, whether it was leniency or immunity. Nine days afterwards, without there having been any long-term interrogation, without there having been subsequent debriefings, without there having been any of the factors which we see in the Lonetree case, some nine days later, a separate intelligence officer came on board the ship and again obtained incriminating statements from Whipple. The court held that promises need not be made, that if a reasonable person implied or inferred that there was some benefit, and if it was clear from the record, as it was here, that those implications were reasonably believed to have a prospect of leniency or immunity, and that implication induced statements, then the statements could not be used in evidence.

We have a situation in which Sergeant Lonetree, for days at a time, for hours on end, was told that he might be a double agent, that he might be able, if he was forthcoming, if he was honest, if he told all he knew as quickly as he could, that he might be able to qualify, that he might be able to participate in that kind of program.

Here Sergeant Lonetree relied on and could only rely on the advice, the faulty advice, the defective advice, the deceptive advice deliberately given to him by an agent of our government, who thought the ends justified the means and, therefore, that it was acceptable, that it was proper to deceive and withhold information from Sergeant Lonetree concerning his legal rights.

Kunstler spoke next:

You can't exempt this intelligence agency and say Miranda doesn't concern them; Article 31 doesn't concern them; they are free to do anything they want. That isn't what the law says. We're all bound by the law, that agency and every other agency, but the attempt, the rote statements, are carefully rehearsed by all of them. They all said the same thing, Little John and Big John. You remember what they said: we're not law enforcement people, we were taking it for intelligence purposes only.

Then why did they turn it over to NIS? Why were the cables given to NIS? Why was NIS given the whole panoply of what happened so they could do their questioning based on what they already knew had been acquired by Big John and Little John?

The law is Ruppert, and Ruppert has been upheld constantly in our state and every other state. There is no deviation. Our motion is a mandate; you must grant it. If you don't grant it, it's simply ignoring the law and saying, I'm not going to do it.

The date was August 5. The suppression portion of the court-martial had lasted since July 22. Judge Roberts made his critical ruling before a hushed courtroom at three in the afternoon, rain and thunder beating down outside.

Roberts, that pleasant expression still on his face, didn't even bother to comment on our "indivisible entity" argument, concentrating instead on the fact that Clayton made his statements "voluntarily."

There has been a lot of evidence presented on this particular motion. A lot of argument. It's taken several days. Basically, we're dealing with the question of whether the accused's confession should be considered as evidence against him. Confessions are not illegal, per se. They have been and are widely used as evidence in cases. Many times cases that cannot be proved otherwise can be proved by the confession of the accused.

Of course confessions in the abstract were not "illegal, *per se.*" Did Roberts think he was instructing a high school civics class in the rudiments of law? But if ever confessions *in fact* were illegal, *per se,* those of Clayton Lonetree—duped, misled, badgered and enticed—would be hard to beat.

To the surprise of no one at the defense table, Roberts allowed the confessions in evidence.

Well, we still had a court-martial to try, and we still believed we could show, with or without the confessions, that quite simply Clayton had done nothing harmful to his country, and certainly nothing approaching deliberate espionage.

17

CLAYTON'S CONFINEMENT

The civilian defense team lived together at three different locations over the course of the court-martial. After separate rooms at the Holiday Inn proved too costly for our shoestring budget, we accepted the generous offer of noted Alexandria, Virginia attorney Phil Hershkop to share his home. But not feeling right about having responsibility for the house when Hershkop had to be away, we finally rented a small one-bedroom apartment outside the Quantico gate.

Kunstler and Stuhff slept on bunk beds in the bedroom, I slept on a couch in the living room, and Paul Stuhff, the attorney's sixteen-year-old son who had joined us to help, bedded down on the floor.

I was the first to get up each morning and would cook up a batch of oatmeal for the group. Then it was up and at 'em, everyone bumping into each other in the close quarters, trudging about in sleepy fogs in preparation for another day in court.

"These may seem like dark times," Kunstler said during one late-night strategy session, "but some day you'll look at them as being among the most exciting of your lives."

Thanks, Bill, I'm still waiting. No, actually, it *was* exciting. Frustrating, maddening, *and* exciting.

Actually, Kunstler didn't try to impress any of us. If he felt like wearing shorts, he did, with casual disregard for showing his World War II bayonet scar.

After Judge Roberts had shot down every single defense motion, he also refused to release the young Indian from confinement. Clayton had yet to be convicted of anything, and we distributed a printed release to the press calling attention to our client's plight.

Of course, the press, dozens of them looking for stories at Quantico, twenty to thirty cameramen each day, had no direct access to Clayton, and because of the frequent blacking of TV screens for "national security" reasons they could hardly gain a true picture of what was going on.

But the public, we decided, had to be informed of Clayton's treatment.

For more than seven months, our release stated, the government had kept him in debilitating solitary confinement, despite a Supreme Court edict that more than thirty days of such incarceration amounted to cruel and unusual punishment. During this period they forced Clayton to eat most meals in his cell; prohibited exercise and socializing with, or even talking to, other inmates; and monitored him day and night by closed-circuit television. He was not permitted, until August, more than half a year since the start of his incarceration, to attend religious services or have any visitors, save his immediate family and his attorneys. Moreover, although high-ranking government officials publicly castigated him, he had been allowed no access to the media for a response. Confined to a 5-by-10-foot windowless cubicle for twenty-three hours a day on days when he didn't appear in court, he was for a considerable length of time prohibited access to television, radio, and newspapers. His jailers monitored all telephone calls, even those to his family and attorneys.

What does a lengthy stretch of solitary confinement do to a man? In an attempt to obtain Clayton's release simply on humanitarian grounds, Kunstler called the young Native American to the stand. As fully expected, he appeared confused and disoriented, anything but a mastermind spy too dangerous to release.

KUNSTLER: Sergeant Lonetree, when did you first come to the brig? Do you remember the date?

LONETREE: The 31st of December 1986.

KUNSTLER: The television monitors, are they on all day long and all night long?

LONETREE: Yes, sir.

KUNSTLER: Since you've been in the brig, have you ever exercised with any other inmates?

LONETREE: No, I haven't.

KUNSTLER: And the exercise that you are permitted to do, it's all solitary, you have to do it yourself?

LONETREE: Yes, sir.

KUNSTLER: Now, with reference to eating, how long did you take meals solely in your cell?

LONETREE: Well, until this weekend, the past weekend, I've ate all my meals in my cell.

KUNSTLER: What happened this past weekend?

LONETREE: I was allowed the privilege to eat in the dining facility with the other inmates.

KUNSTLER: When you say with the other inmates, were you seated with the other inmates?

LONETREE: No, I wasn't.

KUNSTLER: How were you seated in the dining room?

LONETREE: I was seated at a separate table with a guard nearby.

KUNSTLER: Was anybody else eating at your table?

LONETREE: Sometimes a guard, that's about all.

KUNSTLER: And that started, you say, just this past weekend?

LONETREE: Yes, sir.

KUNSTLER: And, did you receive any instructions as to whether you could speak to other inmates?

LONETREE: I was told not to.

KUNSTLER: With reference to other inmates in the brig, have any other inmates been placed next to your cell in the immediate adjoining cell?

LONETREE: No, sir.

KUNSTLER: What's the nearest anyone has been to you as far as cell location?

LONETREE: Well, when Corporal Bracy was here, we were six cells apart from each other, and after he left, a couple of people had passed through and they were in the same cell, and until just yesterday there was another person who was about two cells away.

KUNSTLER: With reference to all the time you've been there, other than coming to court, with the exception of those three meals you mentioned last week, you've been in your cell 23 hours a day?

LONETREE: Yes, sir.

KUNSTLER: Can you give the court the hours that your radio is made available?

LONETREE: Nine A.M. till ten A.M.

KUNSTLER: On what days of the week?

LONETREE: Mondays, Wednesdays, and Fridays.

KUNSTLER: I take it that during the past several weeks at least, you've been here on those days between nine and ten, in the courtroom?

LONETREE: Yes, sir.

KUNSTLER: Except for the three meals you described, since you've come here, every other meal has been taken in your cell?

LONETREE: Yes, sir.

KUNSTLER: And this cell that you're in, does it have windows?

LONETREE: No, it does not.

KUNSTLER: What religion are you, Sergeant Lonetree?

LONETREE: I'm a Protestant, sir.

KUNSTLER: Have you asked to attend religious services?

LONETREE: Yes, sir.

KUNSTLER: When did you first ask?

LONETREE: Well, sir, I can't remember, but I was told I was going to stay in the cell. If I needed it, the chaplain was going to come by and see me if I wanted to speak to the chaplain.

KUNSTLER: With reference to telephone calls, you've heard us indicate there was a guard standing at your end. Will you tell the court when that started, and if it still exists?

LONETREE: Well, sir, until the trial started, there had been a guard listening, and I've been advised that the telephone is being monitored, watch what you say, no classified information is supposed to be said.

KUNSTLER: Does that include talking to your attorneys?

LONETREE: Yes, sir.

Captain Roberts decided to ask a few questions, producing one of the more sadly revealing moments of the court-martial.

ROBERTS: Would you like to get out more in the general detainee population for inside exercise?

LONETREE: I would prefer not at this time, sir.

At first we couldn't believe our ears. Clayton was turning down such a chance? The whole purpose of calling him had been to gain his freedom, or at least to alleviate the stifling solitary confinement.

As Roberts continued to question, Clayton politely raised his hand, like a child in school.

LONETREE: I would like to take something back I said earlier, sir. I would like to associate with some more people.

ROBERTS: You mean with respect to indoor recreation?

LONETREE: Yes, sir.

ROBERTS: Do you feel fearful that you might be harmed by some of the other detainees, if you are allowed to socialize with them?

LONETREE: No, sir.

ROBERTS: Have you received any threats from anybody since you've been there?

LONETREE: No, sir.

When Clayton stepped down, Kunstler addressed Phillip Roberts: "I want to make one observation, Judge. Watching Sergeant Lonetree, and this is the first time I have seen him on the stand, I can see what the effect of eight months of solitary confinement can do. You saw it yourself. This hermitizing that occurs is one of the things the Supreme Court pointed out. You become reclusive because of it. You don't talk to anyone and you are alone.

And you heard him and you saw him. I wanted to point out that I was shocked by it. I just wanted you to know how I feel."

Certainly my eyes and ears were opened by what I witnessed. Talking with Clayton every day, one on one, I had found him withdrawn and curiously passive, but his disorientation was so much clearer when he spoke to the court. Almost pitiful. When he momentarily forgot the purpose for which he testified, and said he wanted to remain in solitary, the amazement in the courtroom was palpable.

Maybe at that point he really wanted to be kept in solitary; maybe he'd made a Freudian slip. (Even though Clayton had answered in the negative to both of Judge Roberts's questions about fear of physical abuse, I had to recall what Clayton had told me about his reception inside the brig.) Whatever, Judge Roberts, in effect, kept him there.

Roberts ruled that Clayton could exercise briefly with the brig population, and eat his meals in the brig dining room, but the rest of the time he had to remain alone in his cell. Roberts also permitted Clayton limited use of a radio.

18

TRUST

On August 10, 1987, at ten A.M., the ten court members—the military jury—were seated, and Major Beck read the charges.

Next came a lengthy *voir dire,* the questioning of jurors for bias. In a civilian court, prospective jurors are examined under *voir dire,* with the defense under virtually no limitations to dismiss; in a general court-martial the chosen court members are subject to *voir dire,* with a maximum of two subject to dismissal. The net effect for our defense, then, was to reduce the number of members from ten to eight. Next Judge Roberts appointed Lt. Col. James P. Allen, Jr., a black man, to the position of "president of the court"—the equivalent of a jury foreman.

With the "confessions" admitted into evidence, the defense held little hope for victory, but getting Lieutenant Colonel Allen as president was a plus. During the *voir dire* Stuhff had brought out that Allen himself had been a victim of racial prejudice, a fact that might augur compassion for our client.

Major Beck delivered the opening statement for the prosecution, starting on a patriotic note by reciting Clayton's oath of duty:

> I, Clayton J. Lonetree, do solemnly swear that I will support and defend the Constitution of the United

States, against all enemies foreign and domestic, that I will bear true faith and allegiance to the same, and that I will obey the orders of the President of the United States and the officers appointed above me, according to regulation and the Uniform Code of Military Justice, so help me God.

Beck's tactic was obvious. We were hoping to show Clayton to the court as no hardened traitor, but a gullible victim. The prosecutor was appealing to the esprit of his fellow Marines. His recital of Clayton's oath implied that sitting before them was one of their own who had betrayed the Corps. Right away he put the government's case on an emotional roll.

We had plenty of emotion on our side, too: Clayton's childhood—the boy as father to the man; the Corps' poor decision to make him a Marine guard; his entrapment by a Soviet woman, and the fact that others had been entrapped too and weren't on trial facing a life sentence. And most importantly, the clear evidence that he had not committed a major crime, that the government had used him as a scapegoat to camouflage serious offenses by his superiors.

The court members listened raptly to Beck's opening argument. They even took notes, like graduate students listening to a last critical lecture before taking examinations that would determine whether they received their degree. I wondered if they would focus their attention as intently on what the defense said.

They would.

The eight members followed every twist and turn of the case, jotting down reminders, asking questions (permissible at a court-martial), evincing a desire to know that I had never seen in a civilian jury.

The facts the prosecutor set forth in his opening statement more or less coincided with the defense's account.

The first witness of the trial phase of the court-martial was called immediately after Stuhff concluded his opening statement.

Capt. Daniel J. Pollock, assistant officer in charge of the Marine Security Guard School, testified about what prospective Marine guards were taught.

The defense, Major Henderson, asked only one question:

"Captain Pollock, isn't it true that Marines on the Security Guard program must sign an agreement that they will remain unmarried during the time they are in the Security Guard program?"

"That is correct, sir," Pollock answered.

Next came David Shook, Clayton's detachment commander at MSG school. He confirmed that the defendant had been taught all the rules a Marine guard needed to obey, including nonfraternization. The defense didn't deny this, and saw no need to cross-examine.

Edward Napoliello, a State Department counterintelligence officer, testified he had personally briefed Clayton on what Marines could and couldn't do on embassy guard duty. Prosecutor Beck was doing his job, carefully laying an evidentiary foundation to prove the defendant had violated regulations.

Napoliello was not questioned by the defense. His limited testimony was not a matter of dispute.

Andrew Colantonio, an assistant regional security officer in Moscow during Clayton's duty, followed.

BECK: What did you tell the Marines, and other State Department personnel, about surveillance in the Soviet Union?

COLANTONIO: That they were undoubtedly under some form of surveillance during their tour in Moscow, during their travels in the Soviet Union, that they were to report this surveillance if they detected it, and that they were not to take any type of evasive or other type of actions which would bring themselves to the attention of the surveillors.

Stuhff cross-examined:

STUHFF: You had information in regards to a foreign service national, a Russian national, employed at the embassy, known as Raya, isn't that correct?

COLANTONIO: There was a female named Raya who worked in the personnel services section of the embassy.

STUHFF: And she's a woman who had been an employee for some period of time at the embassy, isn't that also correct?

COLANTONIO: She had worked at the embassy, yes.

STUHFF: And you had information of Raya's role as a colonel of the KGB, isn't that correct?

COLANTONIO: I heard rumors from people in the embassy, who joked or speculated that she may have been a colonel in the KGB, but this information was not source information.

STUHFF: Isn't it correct that President Reagan himself directed that she be removed from the embassy?

"But how does this fit into the case?" Roberts asked. "I don't understand the relevance."

"This," Stuhff replied, "goes to the fraternization or nonfraternization policy which was just described by Mr. Colantonio, and to his statements that fraternization between individuals assigned to the Moscow embassy and Soviet nationals was discouraged. It also goes to the double standard."

"No, no, no," Roberts said. "I mean, I'm sorry, but I don't understand. If he says that it's discouraged, I certainly wouldn't want unrelated instances of fraternization introduced, either to rebut that statement, or to somehow bolster the case."

Stuhff's point was clear enough. Fraternization in Moscow was widespread. Why zero in only on Clayton? If the government wanted to convict Clayton of fraternization, the defense had already made it known it would listen to a plea-bargain agreement and save everyone time and money. But clearly the government's intention was to protect others and have the public believe Clayton alone had been guilty, and of much more than fraternization.

Master Gunnery Sgt Wingate, about forty-five, five feet eight inches, twenty-eight years a Marine, stocky but fit, had been the Marine Detachment Commander of the MSG in Moscow during Clayton's tour.

I respected Wingate. In our preappearance interview he'd impressed me as straight: you got what you saw with this old soldier (he wore seven rows of combat ribbons), unlike the slick types from State and NIS.

Wingate verified he was in that infamous picture, with his arms around two Soviet women, one of them Raya, the KGB colonel. "They came over and asked to pose this picture," Wingate said. "My wife was there," he added.

I'm sure she was. But the photo taken by Clayton's friend captured the official attitude of winking at fraternization, and the fact that Raya was still enjoying the privileges of the embassy.

Under Beck's direct examination, Wingate explained Clayton's requirement to report contacts with Soviet nationals. A point we conceded.

It was the sort of testimony that exemplified the substance of a case making international headlines by being touted as a sex-for-secrets scandal of disastrous proportions.

I knew the government's case wouldn't get any stronger, but reporters covering the trial didn't. With their TV screens continually going blank, they had to wonder about all the big revelations they were missing, while in fact all they were usually missing was a witness's age or birthplace.

Fred Mecke was called, and this State Department official reiterated his testimony at the Article 32. The depressing details of a raging black-market and poor security practices—with Marine guards urging improvements to little avail—were again aired in a judicial proceeding.

Darrell Enderlin, who also testified during the Article 32 hearing, said that Clayton was not allowed to give that floor plan away.

Kunstler brought out the plan's total lack of intelligence value. He then took advantage of the opportunity to extract from Enderlin his personal opinions of the defendant:

KUNSTLER: On one occasion Sergeant Lonetree indicated to you that he was interested in going into the intelligence field, didn't he?

ENDERLIN: Yes, sir, he did.

KUNSTLER: And, of course, you'd already formed some conclusions about Sergeant Lonetree and his aptitudes and abilities, hadn't you?

ENDERLIN: Yes, sir, they were my own conclusions, sir.

KUNSTLER: And you really didn't think that he had much aptitude or ability for the intelligence field, did you?

ENDERLIN: I didn't say it to anyone else but, yes, sir, that's what I was thinking.

KUNSTLER: You indicated that Sergeant Lonetree was well liked among the detachment in Vienna?

ENDERLIN: Yes, sir.

KUNSTLER: And that's because he tried to help out other Marines?

ENDERLIN: Yes, sir, when he could.

David Boyer, the Vienna embassy regional security officer, testified that Clayton never reported his contacts with Soviet citizens to him. True enough, nothing the defense could quarrel with. Just another minor charge built into a major case.

Big John and Little John, who had testified during the suppression of evidence portion of the court-martial, came back to be heard by the trial members. Beck questioned Big John about Clayton's coming to him at the December 14 Christmas party, and about his turning the defendant over to Little John.

Kunstler cross-examined, and the transcript contains almost as many blank spaces as questions and answers, mainly because of the government's insistence that as an agent of the CIA Big John had to be protected as a national secret (the real national secret they were trying to protect was that the CIA operated out of U.S. embassies, even though this fact had been printed in the *New York Times* and many other major publications). Much of what does remain is Judge Roberts's sustaining objections from Major Beck.

One new point Kunstler was able to bring out, alerted by my investigation, was that Moscow "political officer" Shaun Byrnes had met with Uncle Sasha after Clayton's arrest. Big John said he didn't know why the "political officer" met with the KGB agent.

Little John's transcript testimony has even more "national security" deletions than Big John's, and for reasons of the same charade. Little John played a larger role than Big John, who hadn't seen fit to pull himself away from the Christmas party to interview the master spy. Mike Stuhff's examination of Little John was a beautiful high-wire performance that managed to show the agents' manipulation of a trusting Lonetree while conceding the technical infractions.

STUHFF: During the course of some 20 hours you met with Sergeant Lonetree, you tried to find out a lot about what he knew, didn't you?

LITTLE JOHN: Yes, sir.

STUHFF: And you had certain assumptions about what you thought he must know?

LITTLE JOHN: Yes, sir.

STUHFF: You knew he'd been in contact with alleged Soviet agents for some period of time, up to a year?

LITTLE JOHN: Yes, sir.

STUHFF: And based upon that, you thought he must have been very deeply involved?

LITTLE JOHN: Based upon that, and the other things he told me.

STUHFF: Based on that and certain other circumstances, the fact that money had been given to him?

LITTLE JOHN: Yes.

STUHFF: You became, as you described it, a confessor to him?

LITTLE JOHN: Of sorts.

STUHFF: He trusted you?

LITTLE JOHN: Yes, sir.

STUHFF: You encouraged him to trust you?

LITTLE JOHN: Yes, sir.

STUHFF: And he sought your advice?

LITTLE JOHN: Yes, sir.

STUHFF: You gave him your advice?

LITTLE JOHN: Yes, sir.

STUHFF: Do you think he feels you betrayed him?

LITTLE JOHN: I don't know how he feels, sir.

STUHFF: He spent some of the money that had come from the Soviets so he would be able to get those presents for Sasha?

LITTLE JOHN: Yes, that's what he told me.

STUHFF: He told you he wanted to continue to find out what Sasha wanted?

LITTLE JOHN: Yes, he did.

STUHFF: And he told you he did not give Sasha any classified information?

LITTLE JOHN: Yes, sir, he told me the things he had given them, which I've already described.

STUHFF: He told you he provided an unclassified telephone list from the American Embassy?

LITTLE JOHN: Yes, he did.

STUHFF: And he also denied, when you asked him about certain specific items, that he provided a number of things, such as compromising the alarms. Do you recall when you communicated that to your superiors?

LITTLE JOHN: Yes, sir.

STUHFF: And you indicated to your superiors that you were not convinced by his denials?

LITTLE JOHN: I did not believe he had told me everything.

STUHFF: Essentially, you were not convinced by Sergeant Lonetree's denials?

LITTLE JOHN: No, sir.

STUHFF: You did indicate that it was your opinion that Sergeant Lonetree was a disappointment to the Soviets?

LITTLE JOHN: Yes, sir, I felt he might be.

STUHFF: Sergeant Lonetree told you, during the course of those 20 hours, he regarded his fellow Marines as surrogate brothers?

LITTLE JOHN: Yes, sir.

STUHFF: And he told you that he would defend them, right or wrong?

LITTLE JOHN: Yes, sir.

STUHFF: You also informed your superiors that Sergeant Lonetree, himself, was self-conscious of his minority status?

LITTLE JOHN: Yes, he was.

STUHFF: You indicated to your superiors that he was a gentle and a passive personality?

LITTLE JOHN: Yes, sir.

STUHFF: You found that he had no pro-Soviet political views?

LITTLE JOHN: None that he expressed to me, sir.

STUHFF: Do you recall having informed your superiors that Sergeant Lonetree knows he had a tough life and feels it's hardened him to the vagaries of life?

LITTLE JOHN: Yes, sir.

STUHFF: And then you followed up by saying, in reality he's a sensitive and vulnerable person whose manipulation by the Soviets, and particularly Violetta, has wounded him deeply?

LITTLE JOHN: Yes.

STUHFF: Sergeant Lonetree described to you how his great uncle had received the Congressional Medal of Honor?

LITTLE JOHN: Yes, he did.

STUHFF: And he indicated to you that his great uncle, Sergeant Mitchell Red Cloud, was one of the heroes in his family?

LITTLE JOHN: Yes, sir.

STUHFF: And somebody that he emulated?

LITTLE JOHN: Yes, sir.

STUHFF: Sergeant Lonetree told you he had no desire to live in the Soviet Union?

LITTLE JOHN: Yes, he did.

STUHFF: He told you he felt himself to be a loyal American?

LITTLE JOHN: Yes, he did.

STUHFF: Basically a conservative loyal American?

LITTLE JOHN: Yes, that's how he presented himself, sir.

STUHFF: You indicated you thought he was perhaps powerless to resist a strong personality, is that correct?

LITTLE JOHN: Yes.

STUHFF: That you represented an authority figure to him?

LITTLE JOHN: Yes, sir.

STUHFF: You also indicated to your superiors that Sergeant Lonetree had told you things he never told anyone else?

LITTLE JOHN: Yes, sir.

STUHFF: Did you know Sasha had met with Shaun Byrnes's predecessors?

LITTLE JOHN: No, I did not.

Although Kunstler had dropped the first indications of this newly uncovered evidence in his cross-examination of Big John, the opportunity to exploit it openly hadn't yet arrived, so Stuhff moved on.

STUHFF: One of the things that Sergeant Lonetree disclosed to you is he hadn't reported his contacts with the Soviet nationals?

LITTLE JOHN: Yes, sir.

STUHFF: And that of course is a violation of some technical regulations, isn't it?

LITTLE JOHN: Yes, sir.

STUHFF: And he felt he might be punished for that?

LITTLE JOHN: Yes, sir.

STUHFF: You thought he came to a greater realization during the debriefing that he had been manipulated by the Soviets, is that correct?

LITTLE JOHN: Yes. During my conversations with him, I think he began to realize more and more that he had been manipulated and set up by the Soviets.

When you live a case every waking hour, you can develop a kind of tunnel vision in which you see your client as history's number-one victim of injustice. When I catch myself in such a state, I often resort to a strong dose of graveyard humor as an antidote to the side effects of debilitating depression.

I recalled around this time the case of Pvt. John Wilson, a British soldier I had learned about who in 1815 was assigned to the Bangalore garrison in India. A believer in abstinence, he refused to drink his ration of rum. This enraged his commander, who court-martialed him for "an act of rebellion." Wilson was convicted and shot.

It helps to remember that things have been worse.

19

A PARADE OF BIT PLAYERS

The testimony of Daniel Devine, a State Department communications specialist, indicated to the defense just how desperately the prosecution was trying to attribute a motive to Clayton's actions.

Why wouldn't they just believe the real reasons? A lonely, confused young man fell in love with a Soviet beauty who entrapped him, and he then tried foolishly to escape his predicament by applying techniques he'd learned from spy books.

Witness Devine testified about several social meetings he had with Clayton in Vienna. While drinking at a disco, they had argued about the relative merits of the Soviet and American political systems. With Beck questioning, Devine said Clayton indicated a preference for the Soviet system.

Capt. Andy Strotman cross-examined:

STROTMAN: Sergeant Lonetree said he felt treated more as an equal in the Soviet Union, is that correct?

DEVINE: More as an equal than he had been in the United States, yes.

STROTMAN: He said he didn't really experience prejudice there, is that correct?

DEVINE: Correct.

STROTMAN: But he did feel that both Native Americans, like himself, and other minorities, had experienced prejudice in the United States?

DEVINE: That's right.

STROTMAN: Now, Sergeant Lonetree did not say he would rather live in the Soviet Union, did he?

DEVINE: No.

STROTMAN: Did he indicate a desire to harm the United States in any way?

DEVINE: No.

STROTMAN: He did not say he wanted to help the USSR in any way?

DEVINE: No.

STROTMAN: What he said was that he felt our system was influenced too much by money and by class distinction, is that not correct?

DEVINE: That's correct.

STROTMAN: As a matter of fact, you indicated you tended to agree with that statement, correct?

DEVINE: Correct.

STROTMAN: Sergeant Lonetree also indicated he felt there was a difference between the Russian people and the Soviet bureaucracy, is that correct?

DEVINE: Yes, he did.

STROTMAN: And the lesson he drew from that was he felt the Russian people were just basic ordinary people, like Americans or like people anywhere, is that correct?

DEVINE: Correct.

STROTMAN: And Sergeant Lonetree is a Marine, and you knew he was a Marine at the time, and you in fact are ex-military?

DEVINE: That's correct.

STROTMAN: Now, if during that conversation that evening, Sergeant Lonetree had said anything which made you believe he posed a threat to his country or something of that nature, you would have reported it, either to your superiors or to his, is that correct?

DEVINE: Yes, sir, I believe I would have.

Next came Karen Cole, an embassy nurse in Vienna who had "monitored Sergeant Lonetree's progress with not drinking and with attending AA meetings."

Ms. Cole's sole contribution to the court-martial: "He said he met people in Moscow although he knew he wasn't supposed to, and he visited them in their homes."

Jan Augustin, a civilian friend of Clayton's in Vienna, could have stepped right out of a poster for the Austrian ski team.

Augustin described a party he attended with Clayton in which the Marine guard got very drunk. "In my car," Augustin said, "he got very afraid and intimidated, and told me he was in great trouble. I had the impression there was something he wanted to talk about, so I took him to our flat, which was only two hundred meters or so from the new Marine House. He said he met a Russian family; and a man, about fifty years old, probably a KGB agent, was putting him under some sort of pressure and demanding information from him."

Augustin told Clayton "to report his problem to his local authorities. He was willing to do this, and called the embassy, and later on, also the Marine House. But for some reason, maybe for his still intoxicated state, he was turned aside."

Clayton sought help from both the embassy and the Marine guards, and was turned away. "He wanted to talk to somebody in authority," Augustin said, "and there was, apparently, no one available at this time. It was four o'clock in the morning when he did that."

Clayton persuaded Augustin to deliver a note to the embassy, saying, "Help me, I'm in serious trouble." A Marine security guard called Clayton, Augustin testified, "told him to calm down, to return to the Marine House, and to discuss the whole matter the next morning."

But the discussion never took place.

Augustin also testified about Clayton's plan to entrap Sasha with a prostitute. Incredibly, Clayton's alleged "phone contacts" with KGB agents (part of the government's fourth charge; see p. 151) turned out to be calls from his friend Jan Augustin! Someone at the Marine House had remembered that an individual "with a foreign accent" had called, so the prosecution decided it was the KGB.

Bettina Swatosch continued the prosecution's parade of bit players from their Vienna case. Even the stone-faced Marines guarding the courtroom doors couldn't keep their eyes straight ahead when the stunningly beautiful, slim, and elegant Austrian—Jan Augustin's girlfriend—took the stand. When she crossed her legs, few noticed her radiant smile.

Ms. Swatosch remembered Clayton talking about buying a dress for his "Russian girlfriend." She confirmed Clayton's attempt to turn himself in, and the aborted entrapment of Sasha.

You really had to wonder why the prosecution felt it had to call Karin Nussbaumer. Ms. Nussbaumer (flown over at taxpayer's expense for her brief and inconsequential moment on the stand), an employee at the Vienna embassy, said she talked twice to Clayton, and that he mentioned having a "Russian girlfriend." Also, Clayton talked about "a man he knew from Moscow he was going to meet." Clayton told her "he just got gifts from him and he would like to give him a nice gift back."

When would the meat and potatoes of the prosecution case begin?

Never. There wasn't any meat and potatoes. Certainly not with the first witness of August 14, John Muldowney, an alcohol rehabilitation counselor from Oceandale, New Jersey, who had worked on Clayton's drinking problem in Vienna.

Muldowney said Clayton had a fondness both for Mussolini's system of government and that of the Soviets. Muldowney, a recovering alcoholic and born-again Christian, recalled that Clayton presented his pro-fascist, pro-Communist views quite forcefully.

Mike Lovato continued the parade. This Marine had roomed with Clayton at Camp Pendleton from October 1983 to May 1984. Lovato told the court that during this period Clayton said "he would like to have been a KGB agent, work for the KGB, because they were a real good spy organization; they were better than our CIA."

Like Muldowney, Lovato had been contacted by the NIS in early June 1987, three to four years after the conversations, and with the press barrage on the Lonetree case at full roar. He testified that he thought Clayton was kidding at Pendleton, otherwise he would have reported the discussion.

Special Agent Moyer, in charge of the London office of NIS, again testified at length. Stuhff's cross-examination made several important points.

STUHFF: Do you recall Sergeant Lonetree told you he was trying to string along the KGB?

MOYER: At one point he did, yes, sir.

STUHFF: You had numerous conversations with Sergeant Lonetree in which he expressed that he gave nothing of value to the Soviets?

MOYER: That's what he stated.

STUHFF: Did Sergeant Lonetree also tell you he was pleased he had gained the confidence of Sasha?

MOYER: Looking at the transcript, I would say he probably did make that statement.

STUHFF: Do you remember Sergeant Lonetree describing to you how he misled Sasha about which floors certain offices were located on?

MOYER: Yes, sir, he did say during the 24th interview that he purposely misled Sasha about certain locations of persons in the building.

STUHFF: And you found Sergeant Lonetree wasn't what we might characterize as a very aggressive personality, was he?

MOYER: I found Sergeant Lonetree at all times during my questioning with him to be polite, respectful, quiet spoken. He was a gentleman throughout our conversations.

Naturally. What job applicant tries to impress the boss with a smart mouth and a chip on his shoulder?

STUHFF: And he tried to cooperate with you?

MOYER: He gave that appearance, yes, sir.

STUHFF: Special Agent Moyer, during the course of your interrogations, you found out what Sergeant Lonetree's impression
was of Violetta's role?

MOYER: Yes, sir.

STUHFF: And you found he didn't feel, or didn't accept, that she
was a part of the KGB intelligence apparatus?

MOYER: That's what he expressed to me, yes, sir.

STUHFF: Sergeant Lonetree also, on one occasion, discussed with
you a little plan he had to set up Sasha, isn't that correct?

MOYER: He stated to that effect, yes, sir.

STUHFF: Special Agent Moyer, Sergeant Lonetree, throughout
the period of the interrogation which you supervised or in
which you participated, maintained that he gave to Sasha
only information which fit into two categories: information which was misleading, or information which he didn't
consider important, for a number of reasons, isn't that correct?

MOYER: I'm thinking very carefully on this, counselor, to make
sure I'm absolutely correct. As I recall, he stated that
he supplied information that he assumed the KGB already
had.

Ralph Lindstrom was called on the matter of the floor plans.
A thirty-five-year employee of the State Department, Lindstrom
was shown a binder containing floor plans of the Vienna embassy,
including some Clayton gave Sasha. Under cross-examination,
he confirmed that if the floor plans were classified by executive
order they would be so marked, and these were not. So much for
the prosecution claim that this easily attainable information was
classified.

Ronald C. Moser, Jr., was clearly one of the more desperate
choices of the prosecution. On occasion this Marine sergeant
served as a "chaser" for Clayton during the defendant's continuing
confinement in the Quantico brig. In other words, he might bring
a glass of water if Lonetree got thirsty. Of course, the prosecution
tried to use him as a rat.

BECK: Will you please tell the court members what the accused said?

MOSER: The accused said the newspapers are bullshit, and he said it was not a female, it was a male that was blackmailing him, and he said he couldn't believe he got in so deep, and he should have turned himself in earlier.

The defense had no questions for Sergeant Moser.

Gary Hardgrove made a second appearance to testify about searching Clayton's room. The posters, literature, even a pair of shoes Clayton had bought for Violetta, were admitted into evidence.

Mary Baver came next. This witness, assistant regional security officer in Vienna, testified that when Clayton checked in at his Austrian post, he didn't report his contacts with Soviets; in fact, he denied them.

NIS Agent Andrew Sperber was called back to reiterate that Clayton had been read his rights. The defense didn't deny it. As it had tried to show time and again, Clayton *didn't understand* that he'd been read his rights, or even that he'd been arrested. He thought he was applying for a job, and that the Article 31 reading was a necessary step in his application.

Another Vienna MSG, Pellegrino Luciano, told of taking that phone call the night Clayton got drunk. This was his only testimony.

Thomas Brannon, the "tell us a lie" NIS agent, basically repeated his Article 32 testimony, and presumably continued to make a more favorable impression on the court members than would have been possible had the defense been allowed to question him on his interrogation.

Next, Robert Johnson, an NIS handwriting expert, confirmed that certain items admitted into evidence—such as letters to Violetta and signatures on forms—had been signed by Clayton.

FBI Agent Lee Waggoner also confirmed Clayton's handwriting. It was getting ridiculous, this stagey effort to make sure that the court knew Clayton had written letters to his sweetheart and had signed certain forms, none of which the defense for a moment denied.

In the case of the next government witness, however, the defense raised strong protest. June Dahl's testimony, we maintained as forcefully as we could, should not have been allowed.

Ms. Dahl, a St. Paul schoolteacher, produced a notebook Clayton had used in high school. On it, and inside, were swastikas and pro-Nazi statements (also, in a contradiction that seemed unimpressive to the court, remarks denigrating the Ku Klux Klan and the South African government). In the context of Clayton's miserable childhood, his fascination with Hitler as an authority figure was perfectly explicable, but Ms. Dahl, bearer of this hoary bit of "evidence," had hardly known Clayton well enough to shed light on, or be cross-examined in, that context.

In any case, none of this had anything to do with the charges. The defense protested vigorously, but Roberts allowed Ms. Dahl and the notebook, thus leaving trial members to intimate that Clayton's "subversiveness" went back a long way.

Later, when the defense tried to call witnesses who could testify as to the character of the real Clayton Lonetree, Roberts would rule against their taking the stand.

20

BARRON, JOHN DOE, AND SAM LONETREE

Clayton's passivity at the defense table, I had come to appreciate, was not for lack of interest. He followed every word of the testimony, passing notes to his attorneys to call attention to inconsistencies, contradictions, and points he felt needed to be covered in the testimony. And whenever I talked to him mornings or during lunch breaks, asking him about this or that, he responded cooperatively and earnestly.

Still, there remained within Clayton a quiet, private core, as if he knew something no one else knew or could understand, something that not only supported his composure but gave him hope of eventual deliverance, perhaps even fulfillment of his by-now tattered dream of acceptance as a double agent.

All this changed with the testimony of the next witness, the author John Barron. The fact that Barron, a man whose books Clayton had read over and over again, had been called by the prosecution didn't seem to bother Clayton. He trusted Barron, though he'd never met him. To the young Native American, Barron was *the* expert on espionage. The well-known writer would clear up a lot of confusion, Lonetree must have believed. He sat with rapt attention, hanging on every word.

BECK: What is your occupation, Mr. Barron?

BARRON: I'm a senior staff editor of the *Reader's Digest*. I specialize in Soviet affairs, international security affairs.

Barron proceeded to recite impressive credentials and background, including a stint with NIS.

BECK: Does the KGB, Mr. Barron, attempt to assess and recruit foreigners, specifically Americans, who are serving in the Soviet Union?

BARRON: Yes.

BECK: And how pervasive is that, the assessment and recruitment process?

BARRON: Massive and continuous.

BECK: Mr. Barron, based on your years of research and study of the KGB, are there certain identifiable steps, techniques, which they follow in attempting to recruit Americans to work for them?

BARRON: Yes. The first is identification of the target, of the prospect, and the determination that there are within the individual or his circumstances, vulnerabilities that would provide a chance of approaching him. The next step consists of a judgment as to how the individual is to be approached. Very rarely does a recruitment attempt involve a blunt direct approach: Will you work for us? Here's a thousand dollars. That's not unheard of, but rare. See, usually, an intermediary will be employed to cultivate the agent to continue the assessment process, and by any one of a number of means to entice that target into a relationship with a KGB officer, who will become the director of the recruitment and the subsequent clandestine relationship. During all of this, the KGB is endeavoring to lure the target into a conspiratorial relationship, to induce the prospect to commit acts the prospect knows to be wrong, or illegal or deplorable, by our mores or our regulations and, at the same time, to condition the individual to accept orders, and to respond to KGB control.

I could feel Clayton shifting in his seat next to me. What his idol Barron was describing seemed right on the mark with his own experience, and Clayton was having trouble accepting that fact. Could he really have been such a complete dupe?

BECK: Would you please tell the members some of the other characteristics they look for?

BARRON: People who are having career difficulties, whose lives are in disarray, who evince an incapability of coping, who are unsuccessful in their social relationships, who are lonely or isolated, who have problems with narcotics or alcohol, or homosexuality, or in their marital relations. No one of these traits may be sufficient, but it suggests material with which they can work, and when they find them in combination, they are encouraged.

BECK: Would the KGB, Mr. Barron, be interested in recruiting a Marine Security Guard?

BARRON: I think so.

BECK: Are you familiar with whether or not the KGB often utilizes sex to begin a relationship with a targeted American?

BARRON: Yes, the KGB does that.

BECK: Are there any recent examples that you know of where they have done so?

BARRON: Well, I think in the United States the most spectacular example is that of the FBI agent Richard Miller, who was enticed into a sexual relationship by a female KGB agent, Svetlana Odorodnikova, and who induced him to deliver to her at least one secret FBI document, and to agree to meet the KGB outside the United States, behind the Soviet bloc.

BECK: Are there numerous other cases that you know of where they've used similar situations?

BARRON: Yes, they entrapped, sexually, the French ambassador to Moscow; they recruited the Canadian ambassador through homosexual entrapment; they recruited members of the German and Norwegian foreign offices through sexual relations, tragic misrepresentations of affection. This has been going on for a long time and it continues, because the KGB finds it effective, despite our presumed sophistication.

BECK: In the case of a sexual recruitment, the female Soviet, would she normally be a KGB officer or what you referred to earlier as a recruiting agent?

BARRON: She would be an agent, not an officer.

BECK: Now, after this agent has begun a relationship with the targeted American, what would you expect the next step to be?

BARRON: Sooner or later, the agent has to introduce the prospective recruit to a KGB officer who is trained to direct operations and who is going to assume responsibility for the case and consummate the recruit.

Clayton sat right on the edge of his seat, mesmerized by the testimony. He had accepted George as KGB, and even Sasha, but never, *never* Violetta. He loved Violetta. Violetta loved him.

BECK: In assessing an individual, if a recruitment were taking place in Moscow, would the KGB study places that the targeted recruit visited, modes of transportation that were utilized?

BARRON: Yes, that's standard and elementary.

BECK: After a recruited American were handed over to a KGB officer, what would you expect the next step to be?

BARRON: The KGB would press the American to perform some clandestine services for it, which both the KGB and the American recognize as illegal, and thereby to draw him into a conspiratorial, illicit relationship. The KGB would also require that the American provide information or perform a service which it knows the American authorities would not voluntarily allow to be transferred or performed.

BECK: After the clandestine relationship has begun, is it customary for the KGB to have the recruited agent provide them with classified information?

BARRON: Yes, or information they know the individual knows should not be transmitted.

BECK: And what is their purpose for this?

BARRON: To induce the individual to cross the threshold of illegality and to enter into a conspiratorial relation, as well as to condition him to do what is ordered, and very significantly, to satisfy themselves that this individual is acting upon his own and not under the control of a hostile intelligence or security service, that he isn't a provocateur, that he isn't a double agent.

BECK: In this vein, Mr. Barron, would the operation of recruiting and exploiting a target, an American, a Marine, be closely monitored by KGB headquarters in Moscow?

BARRON: Yes, particularly an American, and particularly a Marine. They'd be very skeptical about a Marine.

BECK: Would the documents or other information then being provided to the KGB by this recruited individual, American Marine, be sent to the KGB headquarters to be checked out?

BARRON: Yes, immediately.

BECK: To determine what, Mr. Barron?

BARRON: Their authenticity and value.

Clayton's face grew progressively more grim. From the lips of a man he virtually worshipped, he'd heard almost exactly what had happened to him. The young Marine dropped his head onto his arms. Tears glistened in his eyes, and then he began to weep. Not only had Barron described his own plight, but I realized that Clayton—unbelievable as it seemed at this late date—was seeing for the first time that his beloved Violetta had been part of the entrapment.

BECK: Are you familiar, Mr. Barron, with whether or not the KGB, and other intelligence services, operate to a great extent in Vienna, Austria?

BARRON: Yes, it's one of the great grounds of clandestine activity in the world.

BECK: In the assessment, targeting, recruiting and exploitation process, is the KGB interested more in short- or long-term goals?

BARRON: Oh, in long-range exploitation of an agent, of course.

BECK: And why is that?

BARRON: Well, if the KGB can recruit someone who is very young, who can be educated, trained, indoctrinated, manipulated over the years, that individual very possibly can be insinuated into a place of extreme importance.

Since the defense had never believed or maintained that Clayton had *not* been entrapped, we didn't think Barron had damaged our case. We had allowed all along that Clayton had acted foolishly, but contended that basically he had caused no damage to U.S. security.

Stuhff cross-examined the witness:

STUHFF: One of the things you told us is that the KGB is perhaps the most effective intelligence agency in the world today?

BARRON: Yes, that's my judgment.

STUHFF: Not necessarily the most efficient?

BARRON: Yes.

STUHFF: It's because of their perseverance, among other things?

BARRON: Yes, and the massiveness of the effort.

STUHFF: And one of the other factors the KGB has in its favor, it's able to accept defeat and continue forward?

BARRON: Yes.

STUHFF: The embassy in the Soviet Union had for some period of time, until they were withdrawn, a number of Soviet nationals employed there?

BARRON: Yes.

STUHFF: And that was a matter of controversy between the State Department on the one hand, and intelligence and security personnel and the Congress, on the other hand, isn't that correct?

BARRON: I think so, yes.

STUHFF: Basically, the reasons of the State Department for maintaining those foreign service nationals were rather foolish reasons, weren't they?

BARRON: I can't honestly say that. I would say, however meritorious the reasons of State Department might have been, I think the counter-arguments were more important. I do not think we should have employed those people in our embassy.

STUHFF: Well, you certainly disagreed with our utilization of the foreign service nationals?

BARRON: Inside the embassy, yes, I did.

STUHFF: If a Marine sergeant were quite naive, there are approaches that could be made to him that he might not recognize as being from a foreign intelligence agency?

BARRON: Well, if we grant extreme naivete, and an ability to disregard training, I can envision that the prospective recruit might, until he got beyond the girl, think he was just involved with the girl.

STUHFF: Were you aware that the young lady involved in this particular incident had been invited by the ambassador to the Marine Ball and danced with a number of Marines at the Ball?

BARRON: No.

STUHFF: Were you aware that it was considered proper for the Marines to dance and converse with the foreign service nationals, such as this young lady, at the Marine Corps Ball?

BARRON: No. I can understand that it might be considered proper and polite to engage in civil discussion with a fellow human being. I was unaware they were encouraged to dance with them.

STUHFF: So that comes as a surprise to you?

BARRON: Given all I've heard and learned in the past months in my research about what has happened in Moscow, I'm not surprised at anything any more.

STUHFF: You are not surprised any more at what the State Department encouraged?

BARRON: I wouldn't say State Department. The whole set of circumstances surrounding the new embassy there, the newer one surprises me.

STUHFF: The new embassy that the State Department allowed the KGB to be a general contractor for, is that what you're referring to?

BECK: Object to the relevance.

ROBERTS: Yeah, I'll sustain it. Go ahead.

STUHFF: So, conversations with such a foreign service national might not be recognized by a person, such as Sergeant Lonetree, as being part of a hostile intelligence attempt immediately when they occurred?

BARRON: The type of conversations you're referring to, possibly not.

STUHFF: And we've all been young men before, haven't we?

BARRON: I have a vague recollection. A very sweet one, I must say.

STUHFF: And sometimes we like to think that members of the other sex find us attractive for other reasons than the information we may possibly possess?

BARRON: Yes.

STUHFF: Introduced by that young lady to another person, a KGB handler, and yet believing the young lady was not any part of the Soviet intelligence apparatus, would that surprise you?

BARRON: I can see how that would be possible. Again, I go back to the briefings, which I presume these personnel received, and I would have thought they would have treated the subject, but I can see how one who wants to think such could.

STUHFF: A Soviet handler who was not receiving what he wanted would certainly make that known during the course of his conversations or contacts with a person he was attempting to recruit or had recruited?

BARRON: Yes, I would think so.

STUHFF: But the mere fact he wasn't receiving what he thought he should receive, that would not necessarily cause him to break off contacts, would it?

BARRON: Not immediately. If after a protracted period nothing desired was received, the KGB probably would terminate the relationship.

STUHFF: What if the KGB operative thought that he was dealing with someone who could be exploited, who could be recruited, but who was very clearly somewhat naive, he'd give a little bit more slack to that relationship, wouldn't he?

BARRON: Relatively speaking, I would say yes.

STUHFF: One of the subjects we discussed is a person employed at the American Embassy in Moscow for some period of time, who is considered to be a colonel in the KGB?

BARRON: Correct.

STUHFF: Her name is Raya?

BARRON: Raya, yes.

STUHFF: And in one of your very recent books you have an entry concerning her, is that correct?

BARRON: Yes.

STUHFF: It's in *Breaking the Ring,* is that correct?

BARRON: Yes.

STUHFF: Okay. And on Page 217, you indicated President Reagan had directed that she be removed from our embassy in the Soviet Union. The President said, "She's got to go." Do you recall that?

BARRON: Yes.

STUHFF: And nevertheless, she remained until the Soviets withdrew all of our personnel—all of the foreign nationals from our embassy?

BARRON: Well, now, so far as I know, she did. I have no reason to think that she did not stay, but I don't know that she did.

STUHFF: You've had opportunity, in the past, to come upon people who thought they could outsmart the KGB?

BARRON: Yes, I haven't known them personally, but I've known of cases such as that.

STUHFF: And there are people who feel they can do that?

BARRON: Yeah.

STUHFF: Certainly, that wouldn't be a very wise course of action for somebody to take on an agency with that amount of resources and that amount of persistence and that amount of perseverance, would it?

BARRON: No, it would not be.

After Barron had been excused, Clayton apologized to me for his "display."

It was finally time for John Doe—the agent, it will be recalled, who said *he* had kept Clayton's appointment with George. Without Doe's corroboration of Clayton's "confession," the prosecution had no case.

Without Clayton's confessions, the prosecution couldn't even prove he knew Violetta, much less Sasha and George. The prosecution couldn't prove anything, not a single word Clayton told the government. Despite scores of agents combing much of the globe, the prosecution had presented no corroboration of Clayton's "confession." Doe was *the* corroboration.

And Doe had readily admitted he might lie.

There is nothing more to relate of Doe's testimony than has been already accounted. In a cleared courtroom, with virtually nothing allowed for public record, he spun his tales of "observing" George, thereby corroborating Clayton's previously admitted rendezvous with a man he understood to be a KGB agent and—therefore, given the logic of that court—confirming his own treason.

One of the more extraordinary diversions of the entire court-martial proceedings occurred when the venerable Sam Lonetree, Clayton's grandfather, showed up at the trial. Though not a witness, Sam had come to make a statement.

Sam walked right into the courtroom wearing full headdress, complete medicine-man outfit, and carrying rattles and a peace pipe. The court could do nothing but look on in shock. Very dignified, Sam faced north, south, east, and west, all the time chanting a prayer. Then he walked over and brushed Clayton with an eagle feather (the eagle is a sacred symbol of the Great Spirit to many Native Americans) before leaving and setting himself up outside to denounce the court-martial to the press.

By now some twenty-five members of the American Indian Movement (AIM) had gathered outside the Quantico headquarters building to protest the trial. They claimed—and who could contradict them?—that the land on which the trial was being held legally belonged to Native Americans, and that if they, its rightful owners, had control, there would be no court-martial.

The government's reaction to the AIM demonstration was to post a sign specifically forbidding "the beating of drums" outside the courtroom.

21

A FAVOR FOR SHAUN BYRNES?

Witness Shaun Byrnes, a foreign-service officer in Moscow employed by the State Department, was more than a diversion. As far as I was concerned, Byrnes held the key to the entire MSG "scandal."

Byrnes, I had discovered, had been meeting for approximately two years, on a regular basis, before and after Clayton's arrest, with Uncle Sasha. Byrnes had been cabling all sorts of information gathered from Sasha—the state of Gorbachev's health, the key groupings within the Soviet Central Committee—to the State Department in Washington.

But the story went deeper. For four additional years, Byrnes's predecessor, and *his* predecessor, had met regularly with Sasha. The meetings were quite cordial. Gifts were exchanged.

"Who paid the restaurant tab?" I asked in my pretrial interview. (Byrnes had also been trained to lie, under oath if necessary.)

"Sometimes I did," Byrnes answered. "Sometimes Sasha did."

It was like extracting teeth—the man didn't want to give up anything—but I managed to get out of him a very curious admission: he had seen Clayton on several occasions exiting the

Metro and entering Byrnes's own apartment building to visit an American friend from the embassy.

What made this admission curious was something Clayton told us he had learned from Violetta just before he'd left Moscow—that Byrnes, a man she didn't know, had called her three times at the Irish Embassy (where she'd also worked occasionally) and had once invited her to his home for dinner. Why had he been so eager to meet her?

Byrnes, off his admission to me, had observed Clayton getting off the Metro, the same Metro Violetta rode the day of her first meeting with Clayton. Could not, I suspected, Byrnes have told Sasha just where in the train to situate Violetta so she would meet the young Indian . . . and then try to confirm this directly with Violetta?

Why?

Because the scandal of the new embassy was about to erupt. Sasha could have been doing a favor for his friend Shaun Byrnes . . . offering Violetta by way of setting up a distraction from, perhaps a scapegoat for, the Moscow mess Byrnes, as a State Department official, had to know was impending.

By the time of Clayton's trial, the full extent of that Moscow farce had become public. Its foundations were laid in 1972 when President Nixon and the Soviets agreed that each could build a new embassy in the other's capital: the Soviets had to use an American contractor; the Americans a Soviet one. Each side had the right to inspect what the other did. As *Newsweek,* April 20, 1987, observed, "Fifteen years later the Soviets have a spanking new compound on the site of a former Veterans Administration hospital in northwest Washington—a site that happens to be ideal for intercepting microwave communications across the city, as many security experts have warned. The United States, on the other hand, chose to locate its new embassy on the bottomlands near the Moscow River. The new chancery building is surrounded on four sides by taller Soviet buildings . . ."

Construction on the U.S. Embassy in Moscow started in 1979. The Soviet contractor used prefabricated building components, while the Soviets had insisted on solid, rather than hollow, concrete blocks on their own embassy in Washington, D.C. In addition, they had refused to accept any concrete slabs that had been cast off-site.

The Soviet inspectors, of course, carefully inspected everything that went into their Washington embassy. Said *Newsweek* about the embassy in Moscow: "Although U.S. experts were present at all times, sources say security supervision was poorly coordinated, and U.S. counterspooks did not inspect the plant where the concrete beams and panels were being poured."

The listening devices implanted in the U.S. Embassy were reportedly so numerous that when Rep. Dan Mica visited the building he held up a Magic Slate, the kind kids use, and asked, "We'll have to write down everything we want to say on these scribble pads?" And when George Shultz visited Moscow in 1987, political wags joked that he'd have to conduct business while being driven around the city in a Winnebago.

Whenever the defense tried to pursue a Violetta-Byrnes connection, Judge Roberts cut us off, claiming irrelevance. Byrnes testified as a prosecution witness—the only government witness to have had direct contact with Uncle Sasha—in the prosecution's attempt to confirm the relationship between Sasha and Clayton.

BECK: How long have you been employed as a foreign service officer by the Department of State?

BYRNES: Since June 1975.

BECK: Prior to your employment by the Department of State, what did you do?

BYRNES: From 1970 until 1975, I was a graduate student in Russian history at Stanford University. From 1965 until 1970, I was an officer in the United States Navy.

BECK: While you were going to school, either undergraduate school or graduate school, were you ever employed by the United States Central Intelligence Agency in any capacity?

BYRNES: Yes, sir, I was.

BECK: Please, tell the members for how long you were employed by them.

BYRNES: From June until September 1971, I participated in CIA summer intern program.

BECK: Are you currently what is referred to as a language-trained, language-qualified political officer?

BYRNES: Yes, I am.

BECK: In general terms, what purpose do you and others in that diplomatic mission serve?

BYRNES: I, and my four colleagues in the internal political unit, have two missions. One is to try to understand and interpret Soviet domestic political developments for the United States Government. The second mission is to project out, to represent our government and our society to Soviet society, to Soviet citizens, to Soviet officials, to explain American policy, to explain American positions, to get our own point across, to show them what Americans are like, what we think and what we stand for, what our policies are.

BECK: In furtherance of that mission, do you have lawful authorized approved contacts with Soviet citizens in Moscow?

BYRNES: Yes, sir, we do. It's a very important part of our function, which is strongly encouraged by the ambassador, and my superior, the political counselor. I, and my colleagues, seek to develop as many contacts with Soviet officials and Soviet private citizens as we can. The Soviet Union is not an easy place to work in, it is not an easy place to develop information on. Not everything is published on the front page of *Pravda,* you've got to go out and check it. The more people you talk to, the more opinions you solicit, the fuller the picture you have of what is going on in that country. That is our job.

BECK: Do you know a Soviet, Mr. Byrnes, by the name of Alexiy Yefimov [Uncle Sasha]?

BYRNES: Yes, sir, I do. He claimed to work at the State Committee for Science and Technology, and identified himself to me as Alexiy A. Yefimov.

BECK: At the time of your contacts with Mr. Yefimov, did you file reports regarding these contacts?

BYRNES: Yes, sir, I did.

BECK: Did your discussions consist of anything much other than

what you have earlier testified to, things of a political, diplomatic nature, those things that are in the press and issues
discussed between our two nations?

BYRNES: I talked, over the course of my relationship with Mr.
Yefimov, primarily about two major areas. My interest in
talking to him lay in the area of Soviet domestic politics. What
were his opinions about what was going on. What was his
interpretation of a major party meeting. Who was going up
and who was going down in the Soviet political hierarchy.
What was the significance of, for example, a particular editorial in *Pravda* on, say, a nationality question, which is a
burning question in the Soviet Union, which is not a ho-
mogeneous nation. Those are the sorts of things I was interested in and those are the kinds of questions I would raise
with Mr. Yefimov, and with other official Soviet contacts with
whom I had regular contact.

We also talked about other areas and other issues. He liked
to raise subjects that bore directly on the U.S.-Soviet relationship. In the early part of the relation, Mr. Yefimov liked
to register Soviet points on, for example, SDI, that was a
major item of interest. He wanted, for example, to make sure
that I understood, and through me, my embassy in Washington, that the Soviets were very serious in their opposition
to SDI, and the Soviets were very serious that if the President
continued to push SDI without showing any willingness to
compromise, then a price was going to be paid in our bilateral
relationship.

Byrnes's recapitulation of his talks with Sasha portrayed two
important liaison officials discussing major international issues.
So why would Sasha bother with small fry like a Marine guard?

BECK: Now, when you confronted Mr. Yefimov with the question
of whether or not he had been dealing with Sergeant Lonetree, and you said he denied, could you tell from the way he
looked, the way he answered, whether he appeared to be
shocked by the question?

BYRNES: Mr. Yefimov, and this is my judgment, Mr. Yefimov did not appear shocked or surprised by the question. He looked me straight in the eye and told me he did not know Sergeant Lonetree, and had not ever known Sergeant Lonetree and had not dealt with Sergeant Lonetree, and he asked me to pass that on to the ambassador and to Washington.

BECK: Did you know, at that time, whether or not he was lying to you?

BYRNES: I thought he was lying.

BECK: Did he appear to be an intelligent individual?

BYRNES: Mr. Yefimov is one of the sharpest Soviets I've ever met.

BECK: Did Mr. Yefimov appear to be the type of individual who could be easily fooled or strung along?

BYRNES: No, sir. This guy was one of the best, one of the very best Soviets, sharpest, toughest Soviets I've ever dealt with.

Kunstler had been itching to question Byrnes.

KUNSTLER: With reference to Yefimov, you weren't the first political officer who had regular contact with him, were you?

BYRNES: No, sir, I was not.

KUNSTLER: In fact, you inherited him, did you not, from another political officer by the name of Jeffrey Chapman?

BYRNES: Yes, sir, I was introduced to Mr. Yefimov by my predecessor, as head of the internal political unit, of the political section, by Mr. Jeffrey Chapman, prior to his being reassigned to Bonn.

KUNSTLER: And the term that's used, is it not, is that you "acquired" him?

BYRNES: I was introduced to Mr. Yefimov by Mr. Chapman, prior to his departure, so the contact would be passed on to another member of the political section. In that sense, I acquired Mr. Yefimov.

KUNSTLER: And, in fact, Mr. Chapman acquired Yefimov from his predecessor, who was Kent Brown, is that true?

BYRNES: That's right.

KUNSTLER: Can you tell the members how many meetings you had with Yefimov after you acquired him from Jeffrey Chapman?

BYRNES: I met with Mr. Yefimov twenty-two times following my introduction to him in July 1985.

KUNSTLER: And I take it, for every one of those times, there would be a report?

BYRNES: Yes, sir.

KUNSTLER: And Yefimov gave you information which was considered significant enough to be classified, isn't that correct?

BYRNES: Yes, sir.

KUNSTLER: The information you got from him had to do, in many instances, with the interworkings of the Central Committee, the relationship of Mikhail Gorbachev with the Central Committee, and who was going up and who was going down, correct?

BYRNES: That's right.

A high official like Sasha getting down on all fours to recruit Lonetree didn't make sense. Not unless much more was involved. Such as doing a favor for Byrnes?

KUNSTLER: You were questioned about two meetings in particular that you had with Mr. Yefimov. One of them was, I believe you said, on the 19th of January 1987, and one was on the 4th of February?

BYRNES: Yes, sir.

KUNSTLER: The February 4 meeting was at your home, was it not; and the one on January 19 was at a restaurant?

BYRNES: That's right.

KUNSTLER: Prior to your meeting on January 19 and February 4, you, of course, had heard about the situation with Sergeant Lonetree, at least you knew something was up with Sergeant Lonetree, is that correct?

BYRNES: That's correct.

KUNSTLER: So, when you met Yefimov on the 4th of February, at your home, you knew that the same Alexiy Yefimov you had been meeting with was the one whom you had been told had been identified by Sergeant Lonetree as a contact for him?

BYRNES: Yes, that's correct.

KUNSTLER: All right. Now, on the night of February 4, I think at approximately 7:30, 8 P.M., Yefimov shows up at your home per an understanding, an invitation?

BYRNES: That's right.

KUNSTLER: And when he came, he came bearing gifts, did he not?

BYRNES: Yes, sir.

KUNSTLER: And he brought your wife flowers?

BYRNES: That he did . . .

KUNSTLER: But he also brought some other gifts for your wife, Jill, and for Barbara Parro, who was your au pair?

BYRNES: That's right.

KUNSTLER: Right . . . And how long, on that particular evening, was he at your home?

BYRNES: Roughly two hours.

KUNSTLER: And you had a dinner, did you not?

BYRNES: Yes, sir, we did. . . .

KUNSTLER: Now, the apartment building where you lived, the Soviets know where that apartment is, do they not?

BYRNES: Yes, sir, I live in a building in Moscow which has been set aside by the Soviet government for only foreign diplomats, correspondents and businessmen. We have a fence around it and a militiaman.

KUNSTLER: Have you ever seen Sergeant Lonetree in that building, near it or in it?

BYRNES: I believe I saw Sergeant Lonetree in that building on at least one occasion. . . .

KUNSTLER: And with reference to that building, how far away is the Metro station?

BYRNES: The Metro station is about fifty or sixty meters.

Which was as far as Kunstler was able to take this line of questioning. All further questions were struck down by the court, and are absent from the court records, on grounds of "irrelevance."

Twenty-two meetings with Sasha, described by Byrnes as one of the "sharpest, toughest Soviets" he ever met, and who knew how many meetings with Byrnes's predecessors. Cozy dinners. Presents exchanged. Then, suddenly, Sasha, a person important enough to have the ear of the Central Committee, appears to corrupt an American Indian noncom. Why should Sasha have risked such a compromise of his relationship with Byrnes?

But everything made sense if Byrnes, acting under orders from some higher-up, had asked a favor from his house guest Sasha: The favor of setting up Sgt. Clayton Lonetree with his "niece" Violetta, shortly before the security fiasco of the new embassy building was likely to come to light.

The next witness was a superstar in the cloak-and-dagger community. Gartner "Gus" Hathaway, "chief of the counterintelligence staff of the CIA," had been with the Company for thirty-five years. He had been a close personal friend and confidant of William Casey.

I suspected Hathaway, whose service dated back to Wild Bill Donovan's time, made the final decision *not* to use Clayton as a double agent after Sasha's little present to his friend Shaun Byrnes had netted not only a scapegoat but a young man who himself wanted to burn the espionage candle at both ends (when CIA telegrams were flying back and forth between Vienna and Langley over Clayton's plan to get Edward Lee Howard out of Russia). Too bad for the young Indian. Clayton's fate had hung for a while on either being a prized double agent or facing the death penalty.

The transcript of Hathaway's testimony contains even more blank spaces than John Doe's, though it really needn't have. It amounted to nothing. Mainly, Hathaway pontificated about the dangers an amateur spy *might* pose. But nothing Hathaway said indicated that Clayton had caused any damage.

The defense interpreted the calling of this old warhorse, who had seen it all, as an act to impress trial members with the gravity of Clayton's case. The mere fact of his showing up had to underscore the seriousness of Clayton's "crimes."

Sergeant
Clayton John Lonetree, USMC

Violetta Sanni

Sgt. Lonetree receiving a commendation from U.S. Ambassador Arthur Hartman for "outstanding performance" after Lonetree's first year of duty as Marine Security Guard to the Moscow Embassy; standing at left, Top Gunnery Sgt. Joe Wingate.

Clayton Lonetree in Moscow, St. Basil's Cathedral in background. Photograph may have been taken by Violetta.

Photograph taken by Lonetree at an afterhours party in Moscow showing embassy officials fraternizing with Soviet women. On right, Master Gunnery Sgt. Joe Wingate has his left arm around a previously identified KGB colonel known as "Raya."

Clayton's grandfather Sam Lonetree, in tribal dress, and his father, Spencer Lonetree, talking with reporters outside the Quantico courtroom. *AP/Wide World Photos.*

Three Lonetree women hold press conference. From left: Sally Tsosie, Clayton's mother; Alice Benally, his grandmother; and Mae Benally, an aunt. *AP/Wide World Photos.*

Sam Lonetree with William Kunstler, after Sam's appearance in the courtroom. *AP/Wide World Photos.*

Sign subsequently posted in demonstration area.

Reporters and photographers, as close as they could get to the trial.

Sgt. Lonetree with the main members of his defense team. From left: co-civilian defense counsels, William Kunstler and Michael Stuhff, chief investigator Lake Headley.

22

JUDGEMENT

"Your Honor," Beck told Roberts after Hathaway stepped down, "at this time, the Government rests."

As expected, the prosecution had no surprises waiting for us. We would have been amazed if they had.

But we had surprises for them, seven witnesses. One after another, Judge Roberts ruled that *none of them* could testify.

One of our witnesses, Philip Agee, wrote a book titled *Inside the Company: CIA Diary,* about his own experiences as a CIA operative. The book had ignited a firestorm of CIA protest, with Agee denounced for exposing the identities of agents.

Agee and four other defense witnesses were intended to testify about how simple it was to identify CIA agents by using published, nonclassified material available to everyone through public libraries.

In short, Clayton's giving Sasha those three photos counted for virtually nothing. Clayton figured Sasha already had this information, as he surely must have—indeed, as he himself had boasted to Clayton.

In effect, Judge Roberts—again using a ruling of nonrelevance—refused to allow testimony from Agee and the others which would have blown away the misconception that the CIA does an adequate job of keeping its agents under wraps.

On the other side, we also had a legal point to make in calling Agee and others. For Clayton to have committed a crime, Kunstler pointed out, "the Intelligence Identities Protection Act requires a demonstration by the prosecution that affirmative measures have been taken to protect the identities of the agent [such as the ones "exposed" by Clayton]. Our five witnesses will show that no affirmative measures were taken. In fact, quite the opposite."

Still, Roberts ruled against their testifying.

Roberts also ruled as irrelevant the proposed testimony of Dave Smith, a former U.S. foreign service officer who had had a lengthy talk with Clayton in Vienna in September, 1986, before the defendant turned himself in to Big John. Smith would have testified that Clayton told him he wanted to be "somebody," "the star of his family," and felt driven to distinguish himself.

Of course, the defense had held this contention from the outset: Clayton's actions were motivated primarily by his hope, however misguided, of making a name for himself by exposing the KGB.

Nor did the trial members hear an even more important witness, Cpl. Phillip Boone, a Marine buddy of Clayton's I had located at Camp Pendleton.

Stuhff explained to Judge Roberts: "Corporal Boone will testify that he frequently heard Sergeant Lonetree discuss his political beliefs and that Sergeant Lonetree voiced strong pro-United States opinions."

But Boone was never heard, even though Roberts *had* allowed June Dahl, the elderly schoolteacher, to testify about a high school notebook, and the born-again John Muldowney to say Clayton expressed pro-communist, pro-fascist sympathies. Yet Boone wasn't allowed to take the stand to say Clayton was a patriotic Marine.

The defense argued long and hard but to no avail. Bitter bile crept up my throat. I'd nicknamed the pudgy and smiling Roberts the "Pillsbury Dough Boy," and right now I wanted to squeeze him. Hard.

"Your Honor," said Stuhff, with all our witnesses excluded, and therefore with nothing else to say, "the defense rests."

So the time had come, with unexpected abruptness, for closing arguments. We had to adjust quickly to the fact that a trial which had gone on so long was ending in an eye's blink.

But what really was there to argue? The factual disputes were not that great. The differences arose in the interpretation of Clayton's motivation. In the summations (abbreviated here) both Kunstler and Beck eloquently and forcefully went over the facts as each saw them, and from their own positions offered, as lawyers will, a little more.

Kunstler—who like all members of the defense team had grown to care very much for Clayton—spoke first:

> You must decide whether Clayton had the requisite intent to commit a crime, or whether he was a foolish young man who thought he could do what Mr. Barron says you can't do, he could expose Sasha. He could expose the KGB.
>
> Take into consideration that he came forward, no one had to catch him and, if he hadn't come forward, Sasha might be out there yet with other Marines, other Americans, other foreigners in Moscow. He's been exposed and Sergeant Lonetree did that.
>
> I'll tell you this, it took a lot of courage to do. If he had shut his mouth, never tugged at Big John's sleeve at that party on December 14th, and just said, I'm going to put in for transfer, I'm going to get out of here, leave the KGB, leave all this behind, we wouldn't be here today. You never would have known, the prosecution wouldn't have known, the judge wouldn't have known, no intelligence agency would have known.
>
> It was wrong for him not to report, but I submit to you he did not have the specific intent to commit the crimes, except not reporting, that are charged against him.
>
> I think you have to put aside all of the feelings about the cold war, or whatever type of war we are in now with the Soviet Union. You have to put aside all of the stereotypes about that country or this country. You have to do what Sergeant Lonetree told one of his fel-

low Marines, and also Danny Devine: you have to try to understand that only by some mutual understanding can we insure our children and grandchildren life itself on this planet, which is in such grave jeopardy.

If you decide this case on any ground but that you are convinced beyond a reasonable doubt that every element, every material element of each specific crime has been proved beyond a reasonable doubt, if you decide on any other aspect but that, which is the legal standard, then I tell you that some night, somewhere, sometime, you will wake up screaming. Thank you.

Beck spoke next:

The fact that the accused turned himself in has nothing at all to do with whether or not he's guilty in this case.

Defense counsel began to talk to you about the accused's great uncle, Mitchell Red Cloud, an individual who obviously, very, very honorably served this nation. And then he began to talk to you about other uncles the accused had, other friends.

The only evidence of any uncle in this trial is Uncle Sasha, not Uncle Mitchell Red Cloud, and what shame it must be for that name to look down now. Uncle Sasha is a KGB agent who this accused willingly dealt with.

The defense would have you believe he's an innocent Walter Mitty. The defense, gentlemen, has mistaken the fictional Walter Mitty for the real life character of Benedict Arnold, because this accused is guilty by his actions.

And I won't continue anymore because you've been in here a long time. I'll just remind you what I said at the outset. You made an oath and I'm certain you will decide this case solely on the evidence presented to you in this court.

The burden Sergeant Lonetree will bear because of his guilt is not because of actions you will take. He is not in this courtroom solely because he came forward on 14 December. He's in this courtroom because for 13 months he committed espionage against the United States. Thank you very much, gentlemen.

After eight solid months of living the case, after a punishing Article 32 hearing, 2,000 pages of single-spaced court-martial testimony, and numerous evidentiary exhibits, we had nothing more to say that might save Clayton. The trial members retired to another room to determine his fate; the defense stayed close to Henderson's office and waited.

There is nothing more agonizingly suspenseful than waiting for a jury deliberating on a major case.

All of us expected guilty verdicts on some of the charges. Clayton *was* guilty, for example, of fraternization. But that charge, like all of them, should have been thrown out because of the illegally obtained confession, and barring that, the Constitution-breaking testimony of John Doe. And besides, even if upheld, those charges warranted no more than a dishonorable discharge.

From the very beginning I had had trouble getting a firm grip on what the prosecution was saying. While we waited for a verdict, I tried once again to recall any serious crime Beck claimed Clayton committed, much less any major offense that got proved. One of the "crimes" wasn't even a crime: that list of agents found in his room.

I combed my memories of every witness who'd testified: June Dahl and her talk about a high school notebook; Gus Hathaway reminiscing about the old days; Joey Wingate assuring the court that Clayton had been told to report contacts. Nothing. All of it smoke.

Deep down, I didn't expect we'd get one cause to celebrate— not one "not guilty" among all the charges and specifications— when those court members rendered their verdict. The government had gone to such extreme lengths to convict Clayton, not only in arguing their case but in disallowing ours, I couldn't believe they'd permit a screw-up on the last turn of the twisted path.

But I could be wrong, I *wanted* to be wrong, and so I tried to find some hope among the others on the defense team.

My friend Mike Stuhff was the most optimistic. He didn't expect a flurry of not-guilty verdicts, but he didn't share my total gloom, either. "Those court members are extremely intelligent," he said. Mike thought that might work in our favor, having people who could see the case for the hot air it was.

But that was just the point, I thought: Those court members are intelligent. They can figure out what is best for them.

Major Henderson wouldn't commit himself. He expected guilty verdicts, but felt the true test would come during the punishment phase of the court-martial. This Marine believed fairness demanded that Clayton's sentence be very light.

Kunstler's view coincided with my own: we didn't have a prayer. He had done what I considered his brilliant best—and this was not my first time in the courtroom with him—but he'd learned too much over his long career to torture himself with hope. The appeals, he emphasized—we'd get them on the appeals. Justice delayed beat justice denied every time.

I talked to Clayton. He said in a matter-of-fact voice that he expected to be found guilty of everything, and he expected a life sentence, also. In three and a half decades of police and criminal defense work, I'd never encountered an attitude so fatalistic. Clayton didn't snivel, nor did I catch even a trace of self-pity.

And then he showed me that he did in fact want some taste of justice. He shook my hand, as if already in farewell, and said, "Mr. Headley, I'd like a favor from you."

"Sure."

"When this is over, I want you to get my story out to the public."

I told him I'd do that. It seemed very important to him that he not be remembered as a traitor on the pages of history.

It took the court members four hours to deliberate, and when they announced they had a decision, all the main players filed back into the small room that had been a second home for us for a month. It was 21 August 1987, 2105 hours. The room, packed with spectators (no desire on the government's part to bar anyone from this proceeding), was eerily still.

ROBERTS: Mr. President, have the members reached a decision with respect to findings?

ALLEN: Yes, sir, we have.

ROBERTS: Would you hand me the worksheet to examine before announcing the findings?

Roberts perused the verdict. The mild expression he had perpetually worn through the trial remained fixed on his face.

ROBERTS: Okay. Let the record reflect that the court has examined the worksheet and found it to be technically correct and in due form. Would the accused please stand and face the president?

All of us stood, Clayton as stiffly at attention as any good Marine.

ROBERTS: President of the Court, please advise the accused of the findings in the case.

ALLEN: It is my duty as president of this court to inform you that the court, in closed session and upon secret written ballot, two-thirds of the members present at the time the vote was taken concurring in each finding of guilty, finds you:

SPECIFICATION 1 OF CHARGE I: Guilty
SPECIFICATION 2 OF CHARGE I: Guilty
SPECIFICATION 1 OF CHARGE II: Guilty, except for the
    word "telephonic" of the excepted words: *Not guilty*
SPECIFICATION 2 OF CHARGE II: Guilty
SPECIFICATION 3 OF CHARGE II: Guilty
SPECIFICATION 4 OF CHARGE II: Guilty

At this point I felt Clayton tremble, shudder involuntarily. So many guilties. And he had seven more to listen to before Allen sat down.

The only not-guilty involved the charge that Clayton talked to the KGB over the phone, when in reality it was Jan Augustin. They even found him guilty of the non-crime of possessing a list.

Hearing guilty, guilty, guilty shook Clayton, despite his fatalistic expectations. Grimness was written all over the young Indian's face.

But outside, a few minutes later, being led to the brig, he smiled as he passed his mother, Sally Tsosie. This angry and brave Native American woman was clutching an eagle feather in her hand and shouting "Innocent!" as Clayton looked into her eyes.

My mind flashed back to that first phone call three seasons earlier in January, a seeming lifetime ago, when Sally said she didn't trust the military.

Kunstler, meeting for the last time with the press, told them, "Clayton took it like a Marine." He added that certainly we would appeal, and somewhere up the ladder, probably in a civilian court, someone would recognize the injustice, plus the violation of Lonetree's rights, and correct the egregious wrong.

23

SENTENCE

Three days later, Monday, August 24, 1987, the penultimate drama—the punishment hearing—was played out in the courtroom.

A Marine Corps-appointed psychologist, Dr. Forrest Allen Sherman, was called by the defense and testified. Dr. Sherman, a lieutenant commander in the Medical Service Corps, United States Navy, was currently assigned to the Marine Security Guard Battalion. Previous to that, he had served at the Naval Medical Clinic, Quantico.

HENDERSON: Dr. Sherman, on 31 December, did you have occasion to meet Sergeant Lonetree?

SHERMAN: Yes, I did. I was asked to come over to the brig to see a prisoner. It was late. I wasn't told anything about the situation other than it was to be treated as a secret. I was asked to determine if Sergeant Lonetree was in a stable mental state and not likely to need special handling or precautions.

HENDERSON: Subsequent to that time, have you become more familiar with Sergeant Lonetree?

SHERMAN: Yes.

HENDERSON: Tell the members of the court how often you met with Sergeant Lonetree and for what reasons.

SHERMAN: I don't have an exact recollection of the number of times. I probably met with him from the 31st of December through March at least six to ten times, varying in lengths of time from five minutes, very short interviews, to one interview of approximately two-and-a-half hours.

HENDERSON: During this time, were you making professional observations?

SHERMAN: Yes, I was. They were primarily concerned with the current state of his mental health and the possibility of his making some kind of suicidal attempt, or some action that would be of concern to the correctional facility.

HENDERSON: Did you form any opinions concerning the problems Sergeant Lonetree got in and some of the psychological reasons why those things happened?

SHERMAN: Yes and no, because I hear two different questions that you ask. Yes, I did form some opinions about Sergeant Lonetree. I never formulated them to the point of establishing a formal diagnosis because that was not a prerequisite of my evaluation of Sergeant Lonetree. The evaluation was always directed at the man I was seeing at that moment in time, and the potential for acting out. But naturally, because of my training and background, I made some broad opinions.

I think Sergeant Lonetree summed himself up within about five or ten minutes in my meeting with him New Year's Eve. He described himself, when I asked him about his background, as an apple. And I did not know what that phrase meant, but he went on to explain that phrase, because we were talking about his name and his racial heritage. He said he was red on the outside but white on the inside. I think that, in many ways, summarizes a man who comes from a very conflicted background with no sense of foundation, no sense of roots. An individual who does not have an integrity of personality. And I don't mean integrity in the way we'd normally talk about integrity, but a structure of personality that will survive a lot of stress and a lot of environmental impact.

I did not go into great depth as to his personal family background or history, but we talked very briefly about a lot of confusion, and a lot of unmet personal needs throughout his life, coupled with a very strong clinical sense of an individual who had a strong need to make a good impression upon me simply for the reasons of the relationship that was developing between he and I. It was important for Sergeant Lonetree that I think well of him, for no other reason than having an authority figure, having somebody that was friendly, think well of him, allowed him to feel good about himself.

If you want to use a hackneyed expression, the 'I'm Okay, You're Okay' book that was on the popular list, Sergeant Lonetree is an individual who didn't think very okay about himself, and to have somebody justify his existence and indicate he was an effective and worthwhile human being was important to him.

HENDERSON: Did you form any opinions about Sergeant Lonetree's intelligence?

SHERMAN: Again, complicated answer. He's in many ways a bright young man. But on the other hand, there's a sophomoric quality, or there's a quality about him that lacks common sense. I think at times, Sergeant Lonetree has his head in the clouds. He's not, in a formal psychiatric sense, out of touch with reality. But I think he lacks common sense at times and is likely to do foolish things.

HENDERSON: What was the phrase you used when you defined the word "sophomoric"?

SHERMAN: Book-learned, but no common sense; a wise fool.

HENDERSON: Did you form any impressions about the father figures that he had in the past?

SHERMAN: I think it's very important for Sergeant Lonetree to feel there's an older man who respects him or who supports him, very much in a father figure. I think it's significant that one of the players in this whole drama is known as "uncle," very much of a fatherlike figure. I think that's an important motivator and important personal incentive for Sergeant Lonetree.

HENDERSON: Were you able to form any kind of prognosis for Sergeant Lonetree's future mental health?

SHERMAN: Yes. I don't see Sergeant Lonetree evidencing personality characteristics that would lead to a complete breakdown, psychotic process. I think we're looking—if I was pushed to the diagnosis category—more at a character behavior disorder, with a certain degree of longevity, which is implied with that. It was a stable pattern of personality. It has its own weaknesses and own strengths. That's not easily changed, and it doesn't change radically in short periods of time. Through normal development, you can see some maturation and some growth.

In addition, I suspect, although I never got enough evidence to make the diagnosis, I think there's a high likelihood of alcoholism, with the possibility of rehabilitation through some program, like Alcoholics Anonymous. I have seen that work many times. In terms of prognostication, though, social science isn't all that good.

Before the court members decided on punishment, we thought it important they listen to Clayton himself.

HENDERSON: Sergeant Lonetree, when were you born?
LONETREE: I was born in 1961 in Chicago, Illinois.
HENDERSON: Who were you living with at that time?
LONETREE: I lived with my mother.
HENDERSON: What was your family situation in Chicago at that time?
LONETREE: We were separated.
HENDERSON: Do you have any brothers or sisters?
LONETREE: One brother.
HENDERSON: What's his name?
LONETREE: His name is Craig.
HENDERSON: Younger than you or older?
LONETREE: Yes, sir, he's younger.
HENDERSON: How much younger?
LONETREE: Two years, sir.
HENDERSON: Do you remember going to grade school?
LONETREE: Yes, sir.
HENDERSON: Where did you go to grade school?

LONETREE: I started grade school, sir, in St. Paul, Minnesota.

HENDERSON: Who were you living with at that time?

LONETREE: I was living with my father.

HENDERSON: How long had you been living with your father?

LONETREE: I believe two years, sir.

HENDERSON: What happened to stop your living with your father?

LONETREE: Well, my mother came and she kidnapped my younger brother and myself, and she took us to Farmington, New Mexico, to live in an orphanage home.

HENDERSON: How long were you there at that home?

LONETREE: Five-and-a-half years, sir.

HENDERSON: What kind of contacts did you have with your mother and father during that time frame?

LONETREE: Very little, sir.

HENDERSON: How many times would you say you talked to your father during that time frame?

LONETREE: Maybe six—six or seven.

HENDERSON: Was that in person?

LONETREE: Maybe once on the telephone, the rest in person, just brief visits.

HENDERSON: What happened that got you out of the mission home?

LONETREE: Well, sir, my mother took me out—or took us out.

HENDERSON: For what purpose?

LONETREE: To live with her, because my father was trying to retrieve us. She opposed that idea and she wanted us to live with her in Arizona.

HENDERSON: Did you move to Arizona?

LONETREE: No, sir. What happened was, we were enticed by my father for a vacation with lots of promises.

HENDERSON: What kind of promises, Sergeant Lonetree?

LONETREE: My younger brother and I were devoted fans of the Vikings, and we wanted an opportunity to see the Vikings.

HENDERSON: What other kind of things?

LONETREE: Better education.

HENDERSON: Did you go to live in Minnesota with your father?

LONETREE: Yes, sir, we stayed with him for an indefinite period, five years.

HENDERSON: Whereabouts?

LONETREE: St. Paul, Minnesota, sir.

HENDERSON: What kind of father was your father, during that time frame?

LONETREE: He was not an ideal father. He was . . . if he wasn't at work . . . later on . . . well, he just . . .

HENDERSON: Did you see a lot of him, Sergeant Lonetree?

LONETREE: During the last three years, no, sir, even though we lived in the same house.

HENDERSON: Did you ever get in any trouble in school?

LONETREE: No, sir, other than that notebook. I had to see the principal; that was it, sir.

HENDERSON: Does that notebook reflect the way you feel about other races and other religions?

LONETREE: At the present moment, no, sir.

HENDERSON: Did it back then?

LONETREE: Back then, yes, sir. I must be frankly honest with you all, that is really embarrassing for me. I tried to hide that. I had thoughts, during that time, to meet other people, and the Marine Corps was something that had brought me a camaraderie, it's something I really cherish.

HENDERSON: Sergeant Lonetree, did you have a lot of contact with your mother while you lived with your father in St. Paul?

LONETREE: No, sir.

HENDERSON: Did you graduate from high school?

LONETREE: Yes, sir.

HENDERSON: When?

LONETREE: In May of 1980, sir.

HENDERSON: What did you do after you got out of high school, Sergeant Lonetree?

LONETREE: I reported for boot camp two months later, sir.

HENDERSON: Why did you join the Marine Corps, Sergeant Lonetree?

LONETREE: Many reasons, sir. I was ambitious. I was very patriotic. I also wanted to get away from my father.

HENDERSON: What was your father like about that time?

LONETREE: Seemed every time I done anything he criticized me.

He was, himself, an alcoholic. He never—the only time we spoke was when he was drunk—so it was time for me to get away. The service seemed the best opportunity, so I chose that option.

HENDERSON: What were your first few years in the Marine Corps like, Sergeant Lonetree?

LONETREE: Nothing spectacular; just uneventful, sir.

HENDERSON: Before you became an MSG, did you ever think about becoming a spy?

LONETREE: No, sir.

HENDERSON: How would you describe the way you felt about communism?

LONETREE: I was a devoted anti-communist.

HENDERSON: When you were through high school, and your first few years in the Marine Corps, how would you describe your social life and your sexual life?

LONETREE: Sir, I don't believe in fornication. I was somewhat shy, it's true. I was withdrawn. I just held opinions to myself.

HENDERSON: Did you have a real active social life with females in high school?

LONETREE: Not really active, sir. Mainly at school, sir, I was more pertaining to future studies.

HENDERSON: Sergeant Lonetree, do you think anyone else is responsible for these things that happened to you, besides yourself?

LONETREE: Well, sir, I'm not going to blame anybody. It's really somewhat difficult to explain how—it isn't a problem to just walk right in and you say, of course, I'll turn on my country. One of the things, I wanted to help the MSG program—I think they should not evaluate the individual but look at his background.

HENDERSON: Sergeant Lonetree, are you willing to accept the punishment this court awards?

LONETREE: Yes, sir.

All that remained for the lawyers were the punishment-phase arguments. Short spoke first, and with no mercy.

In our after-action report, we may be able to prevent for another 212 years actions like these. But that's the job of an after-action report. Part of the job of this court, in announcing sentence, will be to set an example for another 212 years, so this doesn't happen again.

Since we started a Marine Corps, Marines with problems have served with honor, and very often have died with honor. Some of you have served with Marines and watched them die just like that. But only one Marine has made the individual decision for which he must take the individual responsibility, the decision to betray his oath, his Corps, and his country.

Remember the dramatic picture Mr. Kunstler painted for you on closing argument for the defense? He warned of the horror that you would experience, of the possibility that some night you might, to use his words, "wake up screaming."

Look at your list of those American patriots that the accused betrayed, and when you deliberate on your sentence, ask yourselves, how many people on that list will some night, somewhere, wake up screaming because of what he did? Human targets.

Short wanted life imprisonment.
Stuhff spoke first for Clayton:

I think from what has been presented to you, you recognize it as a far cry from the hysteria presented to us in January, February, March, and April.

Sergeant Lonetree is not one who used pawns. He himself was a pawn and a scapegoat.

What do you achieve by being unduly harsh on Sergeant Lonetree? Revenge, justice, deterrence, punishment? Revenge on a weak person?

Revenge is not a proper or appropriate type of reaction for what occurred to Sergeant Lonetree. And, as far as justice and deterrence, you know there's no Marine who would want to be sitting in the chair Sergeant Lonetree is sitting in. There's no Marine who would want to go through what Sergeant Lonetree has already endured. You don't have to worry that other Marines are going to say, well, that's not anything; I'm going to do it.

This is not a situation where you have a Benedict Arnold. This isn't a situation where you have someone who consciously set out to betray his country.

You have an opportunity to show the world what the Marine Corps is really made of. Perhaps I'm too optimistic. Perhaps I give too much credit to this group. I know others feel I'm foolish for thinking you may consider anything but a rote, unthinking response. I hope I'm not. Thank you.

Kunstler spoke more passionately, hoping to head off what he feared would be a terrible wrong:

Major Short's oration to you was such an appeal to emotionalism, Corps pride, patriotism, scare, panic, stampeding, that I just want to mention a few things to you about it. I've heard it from prosecutors for 50 years, not totally different. I want to point out that in making it, he said a few things which you can take into consideration.

Prior to your verdicts, I hoped you would fully understand that you were dealing not with a sophisticated or vain Benedict Arnold, a major general in the Continental Army, who was referred to by Major Beck in his closing arguments, but with an utterly naive and vulnerable loner, a leaf in the great scheme of things, who had been seduced by a young and attractive KGB co-optee at the instigation of one far beyond the reach of this tribunal, and with whom our government maintained close personal touch for three months after it knew of his involvement.

Today you've had an opportunity to see Clayton Lonetree's tormented soul exposed before you. You watched him as he spoke of his father and his mother, and his years in the orphanage. You must have understood something from that. You must have known what Sasha saw in this man, and how Sasha took advantage of exactly what was exposed to you today.

Now I implore you, as fervently as I can with words, to take the true scenario of this background into consideration in arriving at what you eventually decide should be his fate. To ignore it would be to divorce this proceeding from life itself.

Nineteen centuries ago, St. Paul warned the Corinthians that now there abideth faith, hope and charity, and the greatest of these is charity. It is my earnest hope, my pleading hope, both as an attorney and a human being who shares this planet with you, that you follow this dictate and afford Clayton the compassion, mercy and humanity that separates us from the other species that inhabit the world.

I can readily understand, and you know a little of my background, the agony of the Corps at what it perceived to be a most grievous blow to its prestige and its honor; the 212 years that Major Short spoke about. But given the circumstances of this case, that cannot, in any society which prides itself on its utmost respect for the most exalted of human values, be the hallmark of the measure of retribution imposed upon one of its transgressors.

This young and malleable Marine now stands before you for judgment. You will deal with him in a manner which you feel is appropriate and proper. I can only urge you, with every fiber of my being, to approach your awful task in the spirit of St. Paul and the doctrines of the Master, whose advocate he became so many years ago.

There are indeed few among us who can afford to cast the first stone. And in fixing the punishment to be meted out to even the least of us, we must look into our own hearts and our own souls, and adhere to moral principles that have provided signposts for struggling humanity since we emerged from our shadowy sea-born origins and began our ever so perilous, faltering upward climb, a journey still far from complete. There is little else I can place into the scales you must soon so carefully weigh.

I am sad beyond sadness about what has come to pass in the life of my brother Clayton, whose future has been so utterly destroyed by the events of the last 23 months. Please do not needlessly or vindictively strip him of every essence of dignity and self-respect still left in him. If charity, in the fullest meaning of the word, is our noblest human value, then exercise it fully and freely. We, all of us, accused, lawyers, court, yourselves, will be the better for it, both in the eyes of history and our own.

I will be followed by Major Beck, who will do what he can to put you back on the road of severe retribution. But you will have to live with what you do, in the private wars that go on underneath our cranium. The fights, the struggles, between what ought to be and what is, are so well known that I need not elaborate them here. We all have them, large and small. They permeate our lives. And we know that the answer we make to them is how we regard ourselves in the silence of our own solitude.

Henderson spoke last for Clayton. Maybe, we hoped once again, these officers would listen to a fellow officer.

You heard the government's witness say how valuable an MSG would be because of where he'd be and what he could do. And you heard those people say that was the value the perseverant KGB was after. And the government turns that around and says, yeah, because it happened so long, he must have given them something clearly of value.

Well, that doesn't wash, gentlemen. He was being

maintained as a contact of the KGB. He was being used by the KGB for his future value and not because he was giving them floor plans. The government keeps inferring he must have been doing something worse. You make your own judgments about the things he gave.

Was it wrong? Yes, it was wrong. Should he be punished? Yes. Should he be punished further than the 241 days he's already been in the brig? Yeah. I would suggest probably he's got a few more days in the brig left to go.

But consider what he really did, and not the inferences the government would have you draw, that since the KGB wanted him, it must have been horrible. Well, that's speculation and guess.

You know what he did. You know he was being held for what he could do in the future. And you know that when, as Jan Augustin testified, they started turning the screws, you gentlemen know that's when it was fish or cut bait, and Clayton Lonetree once again became Sergeant Lonetree. Clayton Lonetree acted as we expect our Marines to act.

You're going to send a signal, gentlemen, and you know who you're going to send a signal to: another naive young kid who gets caught up in these dealings. He's the one who's going to get a signal from this, and the signal is going to be: I'm staying right where I am. I'm not telling nobody nothing. If worse comes to worse, I'll get drunk, or backtalk the gunny, I'll get pulled off the MSG program and get sent back to the United States and I'll go to Camp Lejeune, or I'll go to Barstow, or I'll go to Camp Pendleton; and I'll just sit there fat, dumb and happy for either the rest of my enlistment or for 15 years service—which is exactly what Sergeant Lonetree could have done, and he didn't.

Henderson showed guts to argue for Clayton as he did, in terms of Marine Corps behavior.

Beck addressed the trial members last, clearly unmoved by anything the defense had said.

> We ask, gentlemen, that you do talk. That you do consider. That you do remember what was said at the beginning. If, based on the evidence presented, and not arguments wherein things were said which were not presented in this case, you feel it appropriate, you walk back in and look Sergeant Lonetree in the eye and say, "This court sentences you to confinement for the rest of your natural life." Thank you, gentlemen.

The defense, waiting to hear the punishment, gathered in Henderson's office, or walked in corridors or outside. We chatted with the press, trying to be optimistic. Even William Kunstler put on a brave face, despite what all his experience had taught.

The trial members entered the packed courtroom at 1550 hours, 24 August 1987. The press watched on TV from the house on the hill. Sally Tsosie sat stock still.

Do right, dammit, I thought. But the words I heard are the same printed forever in shame on Page 1995 of that cold court-martial transcript.

ALLEN: Sergeant Clayton J. Lonetree, it is my duty as President of the Court to inform you that the court sentences you:

> To be reduced to the grade of E–1,
> To be fined $5,000,
> To forfeit all pay and allowances,
> To be confined for 30 years,
> To be dishonorably discharged from the Naval service.

EPILOGUE

Kunstler and Stuhff were eventually fired from representation of Lonetree on any appeal motion (I was not, though the matter was moot), and were replaced by Lawrence Cohen, a Minnesota attorney and politician, who made his presence in the case known just after the verdict.

Cohen had been mayor of St. Paul and now is a local judge. He was serving as mayor when Kunstler tried the Wounded Knee cases in St. Paul, and the two met. After Sally Tsosie's calls for help, Kunstler, because of the enormous work involved, asked Cohen to help with Clayton's case. He refused politely, citing the judgeship he had just accepted and a need to wind up his practice.

Immediately after the guilty verdict and sentence, Kunstler and Stuhff received identical letters from Cohen, ostensibly seeking a timetable and plans for appeals. Cohen also visited Quantico, where he met with Major Henderson and Clayton. He and Spencer Lonetree visited Bob Woodward of the *Washington Post*, seeking his participation and assistance.

It seemed strange that an attorney who refused to help when most needed, when the work had to be done, time committed, and money raised, would now, in the same position as then, have no problem with other commitments.

Stuhff called him. Cohen said we had established a strong record for appeal. He called Judge Roberts "stupid" for some of the rulings he made.

An important and altogether foreseeable development had arisen: numerous intelligence agencies were clamoring to interview Clayton. The government had still not given up on its theory of a nest of spies flourishing in the Marine Security Guard contingent, and it wanted Clayton to tell everything he knew.

We knew what Clayton knew. He already had told everything (and made things up as well). But if the government didn't want to believe that, fine.

Authorities made their first offer: a two-year sentence reduction if Clayton participated in "damage control" debriefings under an immunity grant.

Henderson wanted to take the deal. Kunstler, Stuhff, and I did not. We believed strongly that the government should agree to much more of a sentence reduction for any "damage control" assessment. Golly, Uncle Sasha's Marine Guard spies might at the very moment be pilfering our country's most secret secrets.

Other more serious reasons convinced us we were dealing from a very strong hand, that a two-year sentence reduction was a joke. We had built solid appeal issues, and the prosecution knew it. A successful appeal, and few doubted we possessed one, would mean a sentence reduction of all thirty years.

Henderson gave us his strongest argument. If we didn't take the deal "they are going to give Clayton immunity and *order* him to cooperate. Then we get nothing."

Admittedly, a tough choice. The decision had to be Clayton's—we made this clear to our client—but we also gave our best advice: participate, if necessary, under immunity in a damage control assessment, but without prior agreement as to sentence reduction; any such agreement would only serve to reinforce the fallacious premise that he'd been a major spy inflicting grave damage; and reducing that horrendous thirty-year sentence by a mere two years would leave the unmistakable impression that the prosecution dealt from strength, when the opposite held true. The prosecution was caught in a bind: it desperately wanted Clayton to talk, but it knew we held the cards in a coming appeal.

Two weeks went by. Stuhff received a call from Sally Tsosie.

She said she had phoned the brig and been told that Clayton had been taken to Washington, D.C., for debriefing by the CIA. What was going on?

Stuhff called Henderson at his home. The Marine lawyer was surprised we hadn't heard. Yes, an agreement had been signed, providing for a five-year reduction.

Not enough, thought Stuhff, not nearly enough.

"Larry Cohen told me you knew about it," Henderson said. "Isn't he working with you? Doesn't he keep you informed?"

Stuhff reached Clayton. He asked us to stay on for his appeal. "I thought you knew we made that deal," he said.

Finally, a call to Cohen, who came right to the point: Kunstler and Stuhff would receive a letter from Clayton discharging them.

And the message did indeed arrive in due course, drafted by Cohen. The two civilian lawyers were out; the considerable work they had done on the expected appeal would never be used. Stuhff speculated that Cohen wanted the glory of playing savior in the expected appeals process.

I didn't know.

But as months marched by, I began to wonder: *what* appeals process? A year has passed as I write this, keeping my promise to Clayton, and there has been no announcement. Lee Calligaro and Lt. Comdr. Louis Saccocchio are supposedly handling Clayton's appeal. Calligaro, now a civilian lawyer, was the attorney in the judge advocate general's office who drafted the charges against Lt. William Calley in the My Lai massacre case.

Maybe another father figure influenced Clayton to dismiss Kunstler and Stuhff. Certainly Clayton had been prone to such an influence before. Actually more than a father *figure,* rather the father himself.

Then, in the Spring of 1989, came the publication of a book titled *Moscow Station,* which was excerpted in a cover story (2/20/89) in *Time* magazine and accorded a segment on "Sixty Minutes." Author Ronald Kessler, refusing to name his alleged key sources (reminding me of Clayton's court-martial, with its John Doe, Little John, and Big John), contends that Cpl. Arnold Bracy was one of the master spies responsible for "the worst intelligence debacle since the CIA's abortive 1961 invasion of Cuba at the Bay of Pigs."

The book clearly represents a point of view. Kessler needed high-level assistance in gaining access to his alleged insiders. Other journalists and authors seeking such access had been shown the door. Since the book is anti-State Department, anti-CIA, and anti-Marine Corps, it behooves one to look elsewhere for Kessler's sponsor. The FBI? In his 1988 book, *Spy v. Spy,* he relates his long-standing and close relationship with the Bureau, and there have been clear indications of FBI pique over the bungled handling of the Moscow embassy investigation.

Regardless of the book's auspices, to place blame on the highly religious Bracy, son of a Black minister, it is necessary to dismiss the government-administered lie detector tests he passed, the results of which were changed by NIS to indicate guilt when none was shown. Most important, the government itself—after a truly massive investigation—admitted it had no case against Bracy.

Moscow Station downplays Lonetree's "role"—what else could it do? his involvement is fully detailed here—while playing the original government tune: inexperienced enlisted men, not higher-ups, were responsible for the scandal. So the scapegoating continues, with a young Black GI exchanged for a Native American.

The Marine Corps, from the lowest ranks to the topmost echelons, has expressed outrage over allegations in *Moscow Station.* Major David Henderson, who continues his determined struggle for Clayton's freedom, was asked by "Sixty Minutes" to appear on its program. Henderson was eager to speak out against Kessler's claims, but Secretary of the Navy William L. Ball III expressly forbade it.

The book describes Clayton as "impudent" while in the Corps, with "barely enough intelligence to fire a weapon" and "unfit to guard a grocery store." Where does this information come from? Clayton was unfailingly polite; he took pride in his Military Occupational Specialty (MOS) of Rifleman; and (a fact conveniently absent from Kessler's book) after his first year of duty as Marine Security Guard to the Moscow Embassy, Clayton received a citation from U.S. Ambassador Arthur Hartman for "outstanding performance" (in the presence of Top Gunnery Sergeant Joe Wingate, the apparent source of Kessler's characterizations of Lonetree).

Surely, though, Clayton must have been a keen disappointment to the CIA. The defense team knew it would happen: with his five-year reduction of sentence in jeopardy should he fail, Clayton told exactly the same story he gave us—the one that emerged during the court-martial—and passed every polygraph test the CIA gave him.

None of this deeply matters to me. What burns away inside is the injustice inflicted on Clayton: twenty-five years of confinement, and for what? Without some benign intervention, he'll be more than fifty years old when released, "his life," as Kunstler put it, "effectively ruined."

Perhaps Longfellow said it best, though the poet's words help neither Clayton nor me: "Most people would succeed in small things if they were not troubled by great ambitions."